The Dancing Couple

Books by Kay Brooks

The Row Series:

Spicer's Challenge
Dreams Fulfilled
Newfound Love

Persistent Intruder
Love Again
Shadows of Déjà vu

Victory Hill Trilogy:

Northwest to Love
Journey Back to Love

The Dancing Couple

Nick and Emma's love story

By Kay Brooks

KDB Manuscripts

Front Cover Design by SelfPubCovers/Frina

The Dancing Couple

First edition, March 23, 2020
ISBN: 9780999600689

All photographs are privately owned by Nick and Emma Nichols, Michelle James or Kay Brooks unless otherwise noted.

Published in the United States of America

To: My husband Wayne,
the better half of our dancing couple ~ Kay

To: Michelle, Sheridan, Olivia and Kamren and
in memory of George Nichols

We've lived a blessed life. Helped hundreds of young people excel in sports; laughed often with family and friends. Travelled much and danced to our heart's content.

We truly appreciate the coaches, athletes, teachers, doctors and nurses who helped us achieve our successes. We are especially grateful to Kay and Wayne Brooks, Michelle James, Jaimie Ashton, Carl Braun, James Eberhardt, Laura Hatch, Micky Tingler, and LeCresa Wilcox for helping us to tell our story and believing in us.

Most importantly, without the Lord, none of this would have been possible.

~ Nick and Emma

INTRODUCTION

My working title for this book was *Living, Loving & Caring* because the more time I spent with Nick and Emma Nichols, the more I realized they live life to the fullest, love each other passionately and care deeply about people.

Then when friends asked the subject of my new book and I mentioned Nick and Emma's name or pulled their picture up on my cell phone, they responded, "Oh! That's the dancing couple!"

Another time, my daughter and granddaughter were at the Spotsylvania Towne Centre where Nick and Emma had just danced in the mall's commons area for a local DJ's *Black Friday* event. Heather spotted Nick and Emma walking across the way and said, "Look, that's the dancing couple Nana's writing about."

So, what better title for a book about a couple known for their choreographed moves than *The Dancing Couple*?

Dancing in sync on the dance floor is Nick and Emma's enjoyment but people and giving back to the community, are their passion.

For thirty-five years, after working nights at Grand Union and Safeway stores, Nick trained teenagers and young adults to excel with the shot put or discus in track and field, or to lift weights in the small Nickel Gym they set up in the garage of their home.

There were never losers in Nick's world of sports. He saw potential in everyone he coached. Some excelled and set records, all improved with practice. I interviewed four athletes – Carl Braun, James Eberhardt, Micky Tingler and LeCresa Wilcox – who trained with Nick. Each spoke highly of his techniques, ending their sessions with thanks for all he helped them to achieve.

Emma worked thirty-five years assisting mothers to deliver their babies at Mary Washington Hospital. She shared many hugs and smiles of joy, sometimes tears of sorrow. Throughout her career, she shared a close sisterly bond with Laura Hatch and others on the hospital staff.

Nick and Emma's love of dancing led to many friendships on the dance floor and during their travels across the country. No person, musician, entertainer or sports figure was a stranger.

It was Nick's goal to dance in every state and visit every stadium in the United States. Their daughter, Michelle, doesn't remember a time when they weren't travelling. She visited over fifty-one colleges in her youth for swimming, track and field competitions and Highland games, sometimes sleeping in the car.

Nick often says, "If there's a beat, we're in the street" and most of their married life, they have danced one, sometimes two nights each week. They look forward to boogieing, twisting and dipping to the rhythm of the bands and performing for the people who enjoy watching them.

Jaimie Ashton captured one of those performances. Her Facebook post propelled Nick and Emma into worldwide attention.

Nick and Emma always look for the positive in everyone and say the key to a happy marriage is communication. Nick readily admits that Emma and Michelle are his first love, coaching and giving back his second.

The Dancing Couple has been a shift from my usual genre – contemporary fiction with a little romance and suspense. I have tried to portray Nick and Emma's life as the love story it is – a special bond between two remarkable people who have touched so many lives.

Everyone that played a part in their life is greatly appreciated and fondly remembered. Some names and other identifying details of friends have been changed to protect their privacy.

Again, special thanks to Jaimie Ashton Carl Braun, James Eberhardt, Laura Hatch, Michelle James, Micky Tingler and LeCresa Wilcox for the interviews. To John Wayne Edwards for permission to use his prints and to my husband, Wayne for his descriptions of Fredericksburg and assistance with the photos.

Kay Brooks

PROLOGUE

It was the Summer of '68. Perfect evening for two guys to grab a burger and ride the streets of Fredericksburg, Virginia. Forget about the tumultuous national and world events of the spring – student protests of the Vietnam War and assassinations of Martin Luther King and Robert Kennedy.

Nick Nichols had a bounce in his step, twinkle in his eye and wide grin. He was on top of the world. High school graduation was behind him, he had a job and life was good.

He and David Goodman lived in Bowling Green, a small town in Caroline county twenty miles due South of the city. They'd just devoured fifteen cent hamburgers at the *Hardees* on Princess Anne Street and were ready to cruise the streets, check out some of the gathering spots around town.

He strolled out of the popular burger joint, saw the shiny blue '68 Camaro with the white racing stripe around the grill and pinstripe down the side and froze. It took his breath away.

Emma Burchell, her red hair down around her shoulders, sat behind the steering wheel. The car was a graduation gift from her father who had bought it off the showroom floor. Much as she appreciated the present and freedom it brought, she had to question whether it was a true reward – her father still expected her to make the monthly car payments.

She and Sue Johnson were also enjoying the warm summer evening and had cruised up Route Three from their homes in King George county. Both chuckled when they pulled up beside the hunter green '60 Corvair.

"Looks like a green turtle," Emma giggled as she extinguished the engine, shook her head at the *flower power* stickers on the sides of the car.

A friendly guy, Nick breathed a sigh of relief when he recognized Sue. He enjoyed the game of flirting but knowing the lady involved made it more fun.

"I'd love to go riding in that pretty Camaro," he hollered from the curb.

Both girls looked up, studied the stocky blonde-headed guy smiling broadly at them.

"It's okay," Sue murmured to Emma, "I know him."

Emma didn't know his name, but Nick had caught her attention weeks earlier on the *Starlight Pavilion* dance floor at Fairview Beach. She'd been impressed with his twists, shuffles and hustles as his constantly moving feet followed the beats of the *Prophets*.

She recalled thinking she'd like to get to know that guy a little better.

Before either girl could respond, Nick had opened the passenger door, invited Sue to join him in the back seat, nudged David into the front beside Emma.

Emma quirked an eyebrow, exchanged looks with Sue in the rearview mirror. She was sure Nick was harmless, but his unashamed take charge attitude surprised her.

She figured if she was driving, she had control of the situation.

"Where to," she mocked.

"How about we cruise a bit then come back to the *Jockey Club*," Nick commented. "We can check out the dance floor."

NICK NICHOLS

Nick Nichols was the youngest of three sons. His father, George Nichols, raised the boys after their mother walked away from the marriage when Nick was eighteen months old.

His full name was Rudolph Massie Nichols, but Nick didn't see himself with a red nose or answering to Rudy. At the age of fifteen he decided to answer only to Nick.

"I wore a thin yellow coat with *Nick* on the back."

Because his father worked nonstop, Nick didn't always have adequate adult supervision and consequently failed the third and sixth grades in elementary school.

He liked football and at the age of eleven, bet a friend a dime that the Baltimore Colts would beat the New York Giants in their 1958 battle for the NFL Championship Title. Little did he know this would be the first championship playoff to go into sudden death overtime, making it "the greatest game ever played." Nick won the bet when the Colts beat the Giants 23-17.

"I picked them because their symbol was the horseshoe and I thought that was lucky."

Over the years, Nick managed to meet Johnny Unitas – "one of the greatest quarterbacks ever to play the game"; get an autographed team ball, and a jersey signed by Roger Carr, star wide receiver for the Colts. He and Emma would hang out at the old Memorial Stadium in Baltimore, waiting for the players to leave the locker room. They cheered the team whether they won or lost games.

Nick spent his first fifteen years in Suffolk, Virginia until his father moved them to "Splinterville", a small subdivision on Maury Avenue in Bowling Green, Virginia.

"The first house on the left at the top of the hill. My older brother, Billy had married Jan, and Donnie, my father and I lived with them for almost two years. When Billy joined the army, and served in Germany, we didn't last too long with his wife."

Nick entered the eighth grade as a shy fifteen-year-old with three shirts and two pair of pants to his name. Money was tight and he couldn't always afford to buy his lunches. One day, the school secretary, Mrs. Duke, called him in to the front office and offered to give him free lunches.

"I said thanks, but I'll bring my own lunch. I brown-bagged until I could buy my lunches.

"Billy Gray and Curtis Eagar ran the *Corner Shop* in town. I would go in and shoot pool. Billy asked me if I would like a job racking balls and I made ten cents every three racks. I worked after school and sometimes by the end of the evening I'd have six to eight dollars."

Since he needed clothes, Billy sold Nick the *Dickies* apparel at a marked discount.

Nick's shyness made him nervous around the girls. When he was thirteen, he attended a Valentine's Day Dance in the

Birdsong Recreation Center in Suffolk, Virginia. Dressed in a sports coat and red tie, the girls flocked around him, asked him to dance but he pleaded he had a stomach ache. When some of the mothers noticed, he was the only one not dancing, they tried to encourage him but once again he said he wasn't feeling well. He never made it to the dance floor.

When they moved to Bowling Green, Nick used sports and his work schedule at the *Corner Shop* as excuses to miss the school's social activities.

But he'd always loved music, especially Chubby Checker, the singer that made the twist popular. Billy and Jan taught him the "Towel Twist" in the eighth grade, which built his self-esteem.

Days later, Billy took Nick to his first sock hop in the Caroline High School gym and left him twisting with the girls. By the end of the year, Nick had danced his way into the hearts of several of the older girls and was invited to the Junior Senior Prom.

Nick swore his class schedule was too advanced for him and he had difficulty passing Mr. Waddell's World Geography class and Mrs. Burruss' Algebra class.

"I was supposed to go to summer school, but I took the money my father gave me and hopped on a bus back to Suffolk. I stayed with Charles Matthews, a friend, and volunteered for parks and recreation coaching a little league team. We won the championship."

That summer Nick discovered his love for track and field when he found a shot put in the recreation supply closet and decided to give it a try. He threw it fifty feet and realized the more he hurled it, the more he liked the sport.

"At the end of that summer, I had to decide between school or the military. I decided on school and came back to Caroline."

Lloyd Gibson coached football, basketball and baseball at Caroline High School and encouraged Nick to play on the football team. He participated for two years.

"Lloyd Gibson kept me on the right track. Taught me when the going gets tough, the tough get going.

"My freshman year, Ronnie Smith and I rotated plays; I also played linebacker.

"During the summer before my sophomore year, we were practicing and one of the linebackers on the team grabbed me around the ankle and broke three of my toes. Kept me out for the season that year. The only other game I played was in King George where I kicked a 47-yard kickoff in six inches of rain."

By this time, Nick and his father had moved into a two-room apartment on Main Street in Bowling Green. His father wasn't working so Nick had to look for means of supporting them.

Stuart Martin, local produce manager in the Safeway Store in town, said, "Nick, you keep your nose clean, I'll try to get you a job at Safeway."

At the age of seventeen, Nick was introduced to the grocery business with a starting pay of $1.50 per hour.

Nick still wanted to keep in shape and walked the half-mile from Bowling Green to the high school just outside of town to kick the ball, run four laps and do pushups.

"My junior year, Coach Gibson said he needed a kicker. Then he said he needed a defensive tackle. I think he was trying to make me a versatile, all-around player. I told him I worked nights and could only come to practice on Mondays. So, Coach gave me permission to practice on Mondays, do a walkthrough on Thursday and play the game on Friday.

"As the season progressed, Coach worked me in as offensive half back. Some of the guys may have been a little jealous because during practice, they tackled me and deliberately sprained my ankle. I was on crutches all week which meant I couldn't play in the game.

"At the pep rally that Friday, Coach announced I wouldn't be available as kicker and defensive tackle. I didn't want to be left out and asked Coach if I could get permission, would he let me kick. He finally agreed. Said if I had a doctor's excuse stating I was fit to play, I could play.

"Dr. Martin had his office in his home, and I will never forget walking up that long sidewalk without those crutches. He said I could play, and that game was my worst night kicking."

Nick made one of the four kicks. Coach Gibson replaced him with another player who also missed his kick. When Nick returned to the game and the holder fumbled the ball, Nick retrieved it and threw it to the oncoming lineman instead of kicking it.

"As bad as my kicking was, we still won that game."

Caroline won the District Title his junior year. They tied for the District Title his senior year.

Coach Gibson also started the track program and encouraged Nick to work with the shot put and discus in the spring of his junior year.

He was State Champion in Shot-Put and placed second in the state in the Discus. He also won a chance to compete in a national competition. The Fredericksburg Jaycees offered to fund his transportation to the competition but because of his work schedule, Nick was unable to go.

Many years later, Nick decided this was Fate's way of keeping him on the right path with his job. If he'd competed, the job, and occupation he held for over 35 years might not have been there when he returned.

Nick was ineligible to participate in sports during his senior year because of his age. George Nichols had moved to Massachusetts to live with the middle son, Donnie, leaving Nick to support himself. He was solely responsible for his rent, car payment and insurance, telephone and food, even his class ring.

"My father was a sporadic alcoholic. Both my brothers took him in two times and kicked him out two times. I said I would do whatever I could for my father, but I wouldn't take him into my home."

Nick took government and history in the mornings, then worked evenings at Safeway.

Living alone, he had more time for himself and drove to Fredericksburg for the popular *dragnets* – dances featuring live bands such as *The Prophets, The Cavaliers, The Blues Machine* and providing youth a safe place to gather. They were sponsored by several of the Fredericksburg churches and considered the place to be seen.

Saturdays and Sundays were spent at the *Starlight Pavilion* at Fairview Beach.

"When I graduated from Caroline High School in 1968, I was voted best dressed and best dancer in the senior class."

EMMA BURCHELL

Emma Estelle Burchell was the youngest of four children born to Forrest and Viola Burchell. She grew up on a two-hundred-acre farm with rolling hills and a pond in King George county. She was born late in her parents' marriage and never had to work on the farm like her siblings, Marie, Howard and Garland who were many years older.

She admits to being spoiled and enjoyed exploring the outdoors.

"I remember when I was six or seven years old, my brothers and I would go sleigh riding on the hills at the back of the house when the fields were iced over. We could go down one hill and keep going up the other." She chuckled. "We were lucky we didn't run into any trees."

She sighed. "You know...we had fun back in those days."

Forrest Burchell worked for the RFP railroad in Alexandria, Virginia. He also farmed the land. "We planted strawberries and beans, watermelons, cantaloupes and vegetables and I helped pick them. Then we loaded everything on the truck and carried them to Farmer's Markets to sell.

"We also raised cows back in those days and my father gave me a calf each year to take care of. It was supposed to be part of my education fund. I had to feed it and then he would take it to the market. I remember when the weather was so bad – sometimes the snow would be up to my waist – I had to get water from the well at the house and carry the bucket down to the barn where the hay was."

She laughed. "By the time I'd get to the barn, the water was frozen to my legs. I tried to do that in the mornings before school – especially if it was snowing – because I knew I'd be stuck inside until Dad or my two brothers plowed around the farm.

"It was rough when my father took my first calf to the market. I cried when I saw it on the truck. But Dad would replace it. He'd give me another calf to take care of.

"One time, I had a cow that was pregnant, and she had problems delivering it. I had to go search for my father and he helped with the delivery. We ended up losing the calf, but the cow was okay, stuck around the farm for a long time.

"Times were tough, but my Mother always managed to stretch the budget and make ends meet."

There was a ten-year age difference between Emma and her brother Garland, the youngest at that time.

"I always pestered my mother, 'are you sure Dad's my father? I don't have the same color hair you do. I have red hair. Why do I have red hair?'"

She chuckled. "Dr. Robins always told me I had the prettiest red hair, but I always responded, I don't have red hair."

Despite the difference in opinion about her hair color, Emma and her mother had a close relationship. Viola Burchell always made sure Emma had what she needed.

"We had a wood stove in the kitchen. My mother would cook cornbread on the stove in those big cast iron skillets. She would also fix squirrel soup. We had to make the best of a bad situation. Our next-door neighbor would take the carp, but we ate rabbit, squirrel, deer. I couldn't force myself to eat the deer unless I didn't know.

"I remember when I was sixteen, I wanted a suntan. I was picking strawberries and wore one of those bathing suits with the open back. I wound up in the ER with sun poisoning and third-degree burns and had these huge blisters on my back. They put a paste on my back and sent me home crying in pain and agony."

That was also the summer a neighbor convinced her mother Emma should compete in the Miss Fredericksburg Fair Contest.

Emma laughed. "I didn't place but got a beautiful blue dress out of it. My mother took me to a specialty shop on Caroline Street. We got the dress, shoes, everything, for fifty dollars.

"When you're a farmer, that was big. My mother always took care of me to the best of her ability. She had already checked things out before she let me do the contest.

"I succeeded in that turmoil and it was fun. But I was shy. I just wanted to pick strawberries."

Emma also had time for recreation and went to dances at the King George Fire House with Frankie Crouse. Frankie's grandmother took Emma, Frankie and two of their friends to the dances every Friday night.

During her Junior year, Emma's father suffered a heart attack. "He was obese with heart issues and hypertension. I remember we were watching *Lawrence Welk* on TV. I came down the stairs and he was sitting in the recliner at the bottom of the steps. I could see that he was having difficulties breathing. My mother called the rescue squad and we tried to keep him calm while we waited. The medics came and immediately tried to stabilize him. His blood pressure was so high, they ended up giving him a phlebotomy – pulling blood out of his vein to keep the blockage down. Finally, they got him stabilized and took him to Mary Washington Hospital."

"Watching them work on my father, trying to save his life, was when I decided I wanted to become a nurse."

"The summer between my junior and senior year, I was working in the printing department at the Dahlgren Naval Base. I had the job because of my father's income. I remember I had to apply, and they came to the school to see how fast we could type and take shorthand."

Emma didn't do as well as her friend Joyce, but she still managed to get hired.

"When I told my father, I wanted to be a nurse, he couldn't understand why I chose to leave a good paying job at Dahlgren for nursing. My mother was okay with it. She wanted me to marry a doctor."

During her senior year, Emma participated in the Distributive Education program in school – students attended school half-the day and worked a skill or trade the other half.

She took Government and English in the mornings then went to nursing school at Mary Washington Hospital in the afternoons. This was before Germanna Community College and the hospital had just started offering the classes.

Emma graduated from King George High School in 1966, finished her nurses training the following year and was hired to work in Mary Washington Hospital in 1968.

One day, Emma was scheduled to work the eleven to seven shift at the hospital.

"They pulled me to work in labor and delivery and it was a fiasco. Apparently, there were supposed to be two nurses working and one called in sick. They had already tried a tech, but she didn't work out. So, they called me. There were six rooms full of women having babies. Doctors were hollering orders, patients were screaming. Some of women would start pushing too early.

"I went to my supervisor the next morning and said if you ever put me up there again, I'm going to quit."

Two days later, Betty Thomas, the head nurse of labor and delivery, pulled Emma aside and said, "Emma, Dorothea White and I want you in labor and delivery. You are a natural. You're our best candidate."

"In 1968, labor, delivery and post partem became my field. I spent 35 years there and have never regretted it."

Nick's mother with Donnie, Nick and Billy.

Nick and his father

Nick at age of 13.

Coach Lloyd Gibson

Nick's High School graduation picture, 1968

Emma with her first bike.

Forrest and Viola Burchell

Emma's High School graduation picture, 1966

Mary Washington Hospital
FREDERICKSBURG, VIRGINIA 22401
EMMA B. NICHOLS, LPN
Nursing Department

Emma at Mary Washington Hospital, 1967

SUMMER OF '68 & COURTSHIP

"Are you guys from Fredericksburg?" Emma exchanged looks with Nick in the mirror as she headed up Princess Anne Street toward Lafayette Boulevard.

"No, Bowling Green. I have my own apartment in the town," Nick bragged. "What about you?"

"I live in King George. But I work at Mary Washington Hospital." She might still live at home but at least she had a paying job.

Emma turned into the lot of the *Hot Shoppes* and toured around the building, waved to friends already there. She didn't back into a parking spot as she had last week when she and Sue stopped there for their *orange freeze*.

She also didn't rev her engine like so many of the other circling vehicles.

Conversation resumed as they cruised up Route One Bypass Hill and turned onto College Avenue into the front gates of Mary Washington College. They roamed through the small campus of brick buildings for dormitories and classrooms and exited out the back entrance onto Sunken

Road, then to William Street. Continued through downtown Fredericksburg to complete the loop.

She'd navigated down Canal Street passing by *Eddie Mack's,* the drive in that served the best barbeque this side of the Mississippi, when Nick said, "How about we head on down to the *Jockey Club*?"

Emma turned left onto Princess Anne Street and coasted toward the *General Washington Inn,* the popular stopping place of tourists passing through the city.

The Inn was also the home of the *Jockey Club*.

She glanced across the street and saw the line of people wrapped around *Carl's Frozen Custard*, another tourist favorite.

Emma parked in front of the Inn and the four of them walked toward the stairway entrance to the lower level where the *Jockey Club* was in the basement.

Neither Emma nor Sue had been to the *Cherry Tree Lounge* and considering the size of the Inn, expected to find a gymnasium size dance hall. Instead, they discovered a much smaller room with a bar, tables and chairs and modest wooden dance floor. A loud juke box was situated in the corner to the left of the bar.

Nick and David ordered cokes then headed for the bathrooms. Heading back to the table, David pulled Nick aside. "Hey, you might have been in back with Sue, but you talked to Emma the whole time. What do you say we switch girls?"

Nick didn't complain. Emma was easy on the eyes but more importantly, he wanted to dance.

When they reached the table, Nick grabbed Emma's hand and immediately moved to the small dance floor. She nervously watched Nick's dance moves and began seeing a pattern. Quickly started feeling the beat of the music and followed his lead.

Nick and Emma's first dance together was at the Cherry Tree Lounge in the Jockey Club at the General Washington Inn.

"You know, I've been to Fairview Beach a few times," Emma said during a break. "I've seen you dancing there. You dance like a pro."

The corners of Nick's mouth turned up. "I learned to twist with Chubby."

Emma's eyes grew round in surprise. "You've danced with Chubby Checker?"

Nick laughed. "Not exactly, but I plan to meet him one day."

He leaned closer and reached for her hand, brushed a finger across her palm.

"So, you've been to Fairview Beach?" He asked. "Skating Rink or Pavilion?"

"Pavilion," Emma whispered as she tried to slow her pounding heart. His charm was infectious.

"I go there as often as I can," his blue eyes gleamed as he continued to trace lines up and down her hand. "Usually every Friday and Saturday night. Once I got up on the stage to sing *Down on Funky Street* with *The Diplomats*.

"I go a lot on Sundays too. Couple Sundays ago, I spent the day on the dance floor, jumped into the Potomac to cool off then went back inside to dance again."

Emma swallowed to stop the thrill that ran through her body then shook her head at his crazy comment. "You really jumped into the Potomac? The Potomac River?"

Nick chuckled. "Hey, it was hot. The band took a break, so I did too. Jumped in and cooled off."

Emma just stared at him a moment. "I watched you there one-night last Fall. You were dancing out on the pier with this girl. I remember it was cool and she was wearing this little fur jacket. You must have some rich friends."

"Not really. I just enjoy dancing to the beat and dance with everybody." Nick frowned. "You keep looking at your watch. Is everything okay?" He asked. "You need to be somewhere?"

Emma's cheek twitched. "I hate to sound like Cinderella, but I need to be getting home."

"I thought you said you worked at the hospital. If you've got a job, why do you need to get home so early?"

"I'm a nurse, Nick," she stated. "We don't always work nine to five. Maybe I need to be at work early in the morning." She realized she might have been a little too gruff and sighed. "I still live with my parents and my father worries if I'm not home by midnight."

Nick couldn't argue with family commitments. He'd done the same with his father.

Ten minutes later, Emma pulled up behind Nick's Corvair. He hadn't wanted to leave it in the parking lot and had moved it to the side street between *Hardee's* and the *Inn.*

"I used to have a '62 Ford convertible," Nick bragged. "It was blue with a white top. Used to be a race car. The engine was a 390 bored out to a 406, and I could go ninety miles per hour in second gear."

"Second gear, huh?" Emma cut the ignition. "Is that why you're not driving it now? You blew the engine up?"

Sue and David chuckled from the back seat.

"Actually, I wrecked it," Nick said matter-of-factly. He pointed to his car. "Bought the Corvair there for six hundred dollars."

Nick leaned over, brushed Emma's lips with his. "I had a good time tonight. Do you come to Fredericksburg often?"

"Only to work during the week. I save the cruising for the weekends."

He kissed her again. "Maybe we'll cross paths again."

The following afternoon Emma returned to Fredericksburg. She had just gotten paid and decided she needed to do a little shopping. Hoped she might cross paths with Nick again.

She saw Donald Beach instead. A good friend, he was going through a divorce, and had just seen his ex-wife in the *Hot Shoppes* with another man.

Emma was a good listener and took pride in being a loyal friend, but after thirty minutes, enough was enough. "How about a drive to Bowling Green?" She suggested to Don.

She wanted to look for Nick but didn't want to venture too far by herself.

She'd heard about the small town but had never been there. Was amazed that its two stop lights and short stretch of businesses was smaller than her hometown of King

George. Large homes and hundred-year old trees lined the northern and southern ends of the town.

Travelling down Main Street, her shiny new Camaro attracted the attention of the local state trooper who tracked her before pulling her over. Burl Pack had already checked her tags.

"Passing through?" Burl asked while Emma nervously searched for her driver's license. "Just want to remind you that the speed limit here is twenty-five," he verified her picture and address.

Emma fought to stop her racing heart. She had never been stopped by a policeman before. Many years later, she joked about the incident with Burl and his wife Carolyn who became good friends.

Emma wondered if it was Fate when she immediately spotted a familiar figure strutting down the sidewalk.

Nick crossed the street ahead of them and was about to enter the corner drug store when he spied Emma's hot looking car.

"Hey," he hollered, signaled for her to pull over. "Come to check the sights?" He leaned against the car, peeked into the passenger window, openly studied Donald.

"You could say that." Emma casually responded. She didn't want to seem too interested and had already decided if she didn't find Nick, it wasn't meant to be.

Now that she'd found him, she didn't want to stay too long. She introduced the two men, making sure Nick was aware Donald was only a friend and not her date.

"Glad to meet you. Hey," Nick leaned closer, rested an elbow on the car door. "I forgot to get your phone number last night. Wondered if you'd be interested in meeting me at Fairview Beach on Saturday night."

Nick and Emma's first date was dancing at the Starlight Pavilion in Fairview Beach.

Fairview Beach is a small community along the Potomac River in King George county. A pier stretched over the water, marking the boundary with the state of Maryland, where gambling was legal. The slot machines that had been set there in the old days were long gone.

The *Starlight Pavilion* was Nick's favorite hangout. He knew the owners Paul and Edith Floyd as well as locals that danced there regularly. *The Prophets, The Diplomats* and many other local bands got their start there.

Bands performed on a small platform tucked against the building while the public danced on the wood plank floor and pier. On any warm summer day, children often played in innertubes in the water while the adults danced.

Nick reached for Emma's hand, helped her out of her car after she parked beside his Corvair in the parking lot. They made a beeline for the pier. Once again, Emma studied Nick's moves and by the end of the evening could follow most of his routines.

During breaks, they chatted while cooling off.

"I'm sure you've seen a lot in the hospital," Nick commented. "Do you have any favorite patients?"

Emma chuckled. "Well, I did have one patient I fell in love with."

"You mean I have some competition," Nick joked.

"Maybe," Emma bantered. "He was one of my first patients. Mr. Rhodes." She smiled recalled the older man with his soft voice and friendly smile. "He had surgery for a pacemaker and anytime I did something for him, he would try to slip dollar bills in my hand. I'd have to keep reminding him I couldn't accept gifts. He was in the hospital for a couple weeks and people brought him lots of plants as well as cards and candy. When he was ready to go home, I asked the head nurse if I could help carry his plants down with him. She said sure and after I settled him in his car, he turned around gave me one of the plants, stuck a $10 bill in my hand and then his wife drove off.

"I remember hollering, Mr. Rhodes, you're not supposed to do that."

She looked out across the Potomac. "I still have that plant."

"What did you do with the ten dollars?"

Emma cut her eyes at him while the corners of her mouth turned up. "Enjoyed a *Mighty Mo* and French fries with gravy at *Hot Shoppes*."

"That's my girl," Nick chortled as he pulled her onto the plank deck when the band started another set.

Because of her midnight curfew, a disappointed Emma left Nick still dancing with the other girls.

Summer became Fall. The air turned brisk, but the dance floor was always hot.

For six-months Nick and Emma dated, keeping it to themselves.

Dates revolved around dancing either at Fairview Beach or the National Guard Armory in Fredericksburg.

When they didn't meet up in Fredericksburg, Nick and Emma often traveled into southern Maryland to *Popes Creek* and *Captain John's* for all-you-can-eat meals and dancing at *Pier Three*. Or to Virginia Beach to dance at the *Peppermint Lounge*, *Peabody's Warehouse* and *Upper Deck*.

Emma thought of their courtship days as their triangle of love between Bowling Green, King George and Fredericksburg.

Now that he was graduated, Nick decided to leave his job at the Bowling Green Safeway and thought about going west.

"Roanoke was the furthest I got."

He had bills to pay and had kept his apartment in Bowling Green, so he found a job working sixty hours each week at the Universal Ball Bearing plant in the city nicknamed "Magic City."

Despite the long hours, he still managed to go dancing on Thursday nights in Roanoke before driving two-hundred miles home one way on weekends to Bowling Green and King George to see Emma.

Emma continued to work at Mary Washington Hospital and by Christmas, they knew they wanted to be a couple.

Then the distributor cap on his Corvair went bad and Nick couldn't afford to replace it.

But that didn't stop him from thumbing his way home, oftentimes managing to make the trip to Richmond in five to seven hours. He travelled with truckers or cars, whoever was headed in his direction.

Emma drove to Richmond to pick him up at McGuire Circle and brought him back to Bowling Green to his apartment.

"Absence made my heart grow fonder, and I realized I wanted to spend more time with Emma."

After several months, Nick left the Universal plant and took a job on a National Linen truck in northern Virginia. At the end of the third week of training on the road with his supervisor, the supervisor said Nick would be doing the job by himself.

"If the two of us couldn't get the job done together, there was no way I was going to do it by myself," Nick complained to Emma. "I've found a job at the Grand Union in Fredericksburg, across Route One Bypass from James Monroe High School."

Closer to home, Nick and Emma continued to dance to the Motown and soul beats every Friday and Saturday night.

Their first concert was in 1969 when they went to see Bill Deal and the Rhondells, Mercy, and Gary Puckett and the Union Gap at the Mosque in Richmond.

"We also went to the drive-in movies." Emma laughed. "Those were the days when the sound system was in the box on the pole and you had to hang it on the window, especially on rainy nights.

"Everybody would sneak people in their trunks. There was always a lot of smooching and fog on the windows. Everybody knew what was going on. But we saw some good John Wayne movies."

Marriage was mentioned but there was no commitment. They decided to give the relationship a year.

One weekend, they visited Nick's brother, Billy, at Fort Meade in Maryland.

"This girl's a keeper," Billy stated.

Nick breathed a sigh of relief. He had already bought a ring from an Ohio soldier stationed at Fort A.P. Hill. "He and his girlfriend had broken up and he wanted to sell the ring cheap. I'd had the ring for almost a year but thought of myself as a playboy and held out as long as I could.

"But when Billy said I should marry Emma, that was one of the best days of my life," he later confessed.

He didn't doubt that Emma liked him but was afraid she would say no to marriage. Her parents called him "city slicker" and he worried her father wouldn't give his blessing.

Emma's brother, Garland, had divorced his wife and had a house on Franklin Street in Fredericksburg. He worked nights and Nick and Emma often stayed there watching TV until Garland came home.

One night, Emma was sitting in the rocker when Nick got on his knee and proposed.

Several weekends later, they travelled to her parents' home in King George to ask for her father's blessing. Nick, Emma and her father sat on the back porch outside the kitchen where her mother worked inside.

"Mrs. Burchell, could you come here a minute," Nick called out.

"Whatever you've got to say, I can hear from right here," Viola Burchell replied.

Nick groaned. He knew she wanted Emma to marry a doctor.

Forrest Burchell gave his blessing, but Viola was still complaining on the day Nick and Emma were married.

Where it all began...Hardee's
Postcard from John Wayne Edwards & You're Probably from Fredericksburg, VA, if.. (Facebook)

Eddie Mack's
"Before the Big Mac" Original painting by John Wayne Edwards

Carl's
Original painting by John Wayne Edwards

Emma's '68 Camaro

Fairview Beach.
Original painting by John Wayne Edwards.

Easter Sunday while dating

Nick and Emma's Wedding, September 27, 1969

Reception

MARRIAGE

Nick and Emma borrowed five hundred dollars from Union Bank & Trust for their wedding.

They were married on Saturday, September 27, 1969, at Potomac Baptist Church in King George.

Money was tight, so they ordered a small number of invitations and to save postage, posted one of the invitations on the church bulletin board. Over one hundred people attended.

"I'm sure everyone thinks I'm pregnant," Emma joked with her friend Faye Bryant. "Even the nurses at work give me suspicious looks, one asked outright if I was expecting."

Faye had married Eddie Bryant two months earlier, and Emma had asked Faye to be her matron of honor. She also asked Dare Wright, Faye's twin sister and their friend Shirley Ballard, to be her bridesmaids.

Faye and Dare's aunt, Ann Wright, had agreed to coordinate the wedding.

Emma and Faye were seated at the kitchen table in Faye and Eddie's new home sharing ideas for the wedding. Faye leaned back in her chair, brushed a finger up and down the side of her glass of tea.

"I'm just offering, Emma, but since your budget is so tight, and we both wear the same size, you are more than welcome to borrow my wedding dress." She paused to let Emma mull over her offer. "I'll wear my maid of honor's dress, Dare and Shirley can wear the bridesmaid dresses a second time."

Emma exhaled a sigh of relief.

"Are you serious? My parents can only give us so much and I've been shopping for a dress and just can't afford some of the prices. To be honest, all I really want is to marry Nick."

On the day of the six o'clock wedding, Nick arrived ten minutes early, but Viola Burchell still insisted he was late for her daughter's wedding. She never gave up hoping Emma would marry a doctor.

Emma's father was unable to be there for medical reasons so Howard, Emma's oldest brother gave her away.

The wedding was solemn; the church was full.

For a couple that enjoyed dancing, there was no rock 'n' rolling or boogieing in the social hall of the staunch Baptist church. After a short reception with cake and punch, Nick and Emma said goodbye to their families and friends and started out as a married couple.

They planned to honeymoon at a hotel on Afton Mountain in the Blue Ridge mountains and headed toward Charlottesville for their first dinner as a married couple. When they arrived at the hotel, they learned all the rooms were booked because of a Duke and UVA football game.

They turned around and drove over an hour to Richmond, finally found a room – the Honeymoon Suite – in the Cavalier Hotel off Route 301 much later that night.

On Sunday, Nick's favorite team, the Baltimore Colts were playing the Minnesota Vikings, so they stayed at the hotel long enough to watch the game.

"The Vikings quarterback Joe Kapp picked the defense apart," Nick complained after the Colts lost 44-10.

Nick and Emma settled in a small basement apartment on Sunken Road next to Mary Washington College. It was a one bedroom, bathroom and kitchen/dining/living room combination. The rent was $95.00 a month and they lived there for five years.

The early years of their marriage, Nick worked nights stocking at the Grand Union. When Grand Union started closing stores, he went to the Manassas store where he worked for two years. From there he went to the Belleview store in Alexandria and worked three nights in Manassas then three nights in Alexandria stocking shelves and unloading trucks.

Emma alternated the seven to three and three to eleven shifts at the Mary Washington Hospital. She had passed her nursing Boards and after a short time on One East, the surgical floors, she was convinced to switch to labor and delivery as a licensed practical nurse.

Over the years, Jane Engals tried to encourage Emma to become a registered nurse, but she wanted to be a wife and mother. She preferred working with people, not scheduling and supervising.

Nick and Emma didn't pressure each other to do more at their jobs than they wanted. Whatever Emma decided she wanted to do was okay with Nick. He didn't pressure her to get her RN and she didn't pressure him to be manager at the grocery store.

"We were okay being the doers. We weren't interested in being the boss."

Their lives settled into a routine and their circle of friends grew.

"When I was working Labor and Delivery, a bunch of us nurses – Peggy Morris, Dixie Bettis and Sandra Boatwright – would work the three to eleven shift together and the husbands would pick us up at eleven and we would go over to the *Hot Shoppes* for Mighty Mo hamburgers, French fries with gravy and orange freezes. We always looked for Gladys to wait on us."

Nick and Emma also went to *Pool Room* for hot dogs. "They had a Chili dog that was to die for," Nick exclaimed. They became good friends with the owner.

Nick chuckled. "He wanted us to take over the business. Said he would give us his secret homemade chili recipe if we did. I've often wondered if that was one of those missed opportunities."

Nick and Emma's passion was dancing, and Friday and Saturday nights became their date nights.

If they didn't go to Fairview Beach, they went to *Coachmen* in Spotsylvania where they saw the *Hot Nuts, Marvels, Bill Deal and Rondels* as well as Steve Jarrell and the *Rotations*.

They also danced at *Shannon's Lounge* in Fredericksburg which was their home base for over forty years.

They put together a repertoire of dance routines – freestyle, Nick's version of the electric slide, a two-step, twist, shuffle and shag – to enjoy the music. They rotated their moves, never doing the same dance twice in succession. They would dance an hour or two, gradually built it up to three-four hours.

They travelled up to Alexandria, Virginia to see *The Fantastic Johnny C*, a soul singer noted for his "Boogaloo Down Broadway" at the Springfield Hilton. Johnny C was there with a table of fifteen or twenty people and when Nick and Emma maneuvered themselves onto the floor, the ladies at the table jumped up and started dancing with them.

Nick beamed. "That's when I realized we had something different."

They also liked to visit *The Hideaway* at Fort Lee in Hopewell, Virginia. One Friday, *The Tams* were performing there.

Nick and Emma mingled amongst the large crowd when Little Red – Robert Lee Smith – suddenly announced, "I'd like to have a pale face guy come up here and show me a few moves."

The crowd started pointing at Nick.

"Come on up," Little Red invited.

Nick joined him on the stage and started dancing; the crowd started clapping.

When Nick left, one of the guys in the band said, "good job. You gave him what he deserves."

"I guess there must have been some rivalry among the band members."

Nick and Emma attended many concerts, most memorable of them being watching Jimi Hendrix destroy his guitar on stage; another time, walking through the marijuana haze at a Bob Marley concert.

Emma laughed. "You'd be in all that fog and could feel the effects within minutes."

They also travelled to Richmond and Virginia Beach. Some of the places they frequented were *Peppermint Beach Club, Upper Deck, Peabody's, Rouges Gallery*, Days Inn. In Richmond, the *Sheik*, Tobacco Company, Holiday Inn on Broad Street.

6600 MILES IN 12 DAYS

Nick's goal in life is to see every stadium in the country and dance in every state of the U.S.

They planned their vacations accordingly. For their first trip, in 1970, they went South and stayed in Miami. Toured the *Orange Bowl*.

In 1971, they enjoyed the fall foliage when they went North to Maine, Canada, Montreal, Toronto, Detroit, Missouri and back across W.VA.

They visited the *Detroit Tigers* baseball stadium and saw Al "Mr. Tiger" Kaline hit a home run. "Hammerin' Harmon" Killebrew, who used to play for the *Washington Senators* also hit a home run for the *Twins* that night.

"One memorable moment was watching Big Al selling his hotdogs and drinks. He kept hollering 'Al's red hots, yummy yummy' over and over as he marched up and down the aisle steps."

In 1972, they travelled 6600 miles in 12 days.

They left Fredericksburg at three in the morning, with Emma's Camaro packed floorboard to the roof. Nick had just been prescribed glasses but thought he was too macho to wear them. As they crossed the North Carolina border, he started looking for a gas station, but noticed the road signs were fuzzy.

"What did that sign say?" He finally asked.

"Put your glasses on and you can read it," Emma scolded him.

Figuring he was far enough away from home for anyone to recognize him, Nick put the glasses on and realized he could see much better.

Emma took over the driving in Alabama and was passing a car on a two-lane highway when they realized an eighteen-wheel tractor trailer was coming towards them.

"Pull to the left shoulder and stop," Nick shouted when Emma panicked. Seconds later amid honking horns, squealing tires and smoking brakes, they pulled off the road in time for the tractor-trailer to barrel past them.

"I'll drive," Nick stated and drove the rest of the way, arriving in New Orleans, Louisiana at nine that night.

"Can you believe we've driven one thousand miles today?" Nick bragged after they checked into their room and headed for the hotel's pool to cool off.

The next day, they toured the French quarters, had lunch on the patio outside a restaurant and watched the construction of the *Superdome* before moving on to Baton Rouge.

In Baton Rouge, they toured LSU – Louisiana State University – and saw the football team practicing. They also took time to check out *Tiger Stadium* – 6th largest stadium in world; 3rd largest in Southeastern Conference; and 5th largest in NCAA.

Early the next morning they headed to Houston, Texas and drove by the *Houston Astrodome* – first NFL stadium with a retractable roof – continuing to Dallas Fort Worth.

They registered at a *Ramada Inn* and visited the *Dallas Cowboys'* Stadium. "The guard let us in to look at the field but forgot to tell us about the guard dogs on the far side of the stadium. Fortunately, we hadn't planned to stay long and managed to get out safely."

Next, they checked out the *Seven Seas Sea Life Park,* a theme park like *Sea World* that had just opened.

Their fourth day, they travelled to Albuquerque, New Mexico, stayed in an old Mexican town full of antique shops and rode the *Sandia Peak Tramway* for a panoramic view of the canyons and terrain of the Cibola National Forest.

Day five was spent crossing Arizona, stopping briefly at the *Hoover Dam* and *Grand Canyon,* on their way to California. They drove US-101 N from Long Beach up to Salinas to see *Fort Ord* army post on Monterey Bay. Visited with Nick's brother Donnie who was stationed at the base.

After an overnight visit with Donnie, they travelled up the coast to Anaheim and saw *Disneyland* and *Universal Studios.* Stayed that night in Los Angeles at a motel named *Vagabond* and saw the Los Angeles Coliseum and the basketball arena at the *Staples Center*.

They drove through Beverly Hills and Hollywood on their way to San Francisco where they saw *Candlestick Park Stadium*, home of the *San Francisco 49ers* and *Oakland Coliseum* – second smallest NFL stadium in the country and home of the Oakland Raiders.

When they crossed the *Golden Gate Bridge*, the car broke down on other side of bridge. The fan belt had come loose, but they were lucky enough to be near a gas station to have it tightened.

In Sacramento, they stayed in a *Rodeway Inn* after visiting two track and field stadiums.

Television and film actress Barbara McNair and comedian Shecky Greene were performing at the *Riviera Hotel and Casino* in Las Vegas and while there, a man walked past them.

Nick poked Emma and commented it was Steve Lawrence, but Emma thought he was kidding. Moments later Steve and his wife Eydie Gorme were introduced to the crowd.

Their ninth day was spent in Salt Lake City, UT where they saw the "Taj Mahal" an abandoned castle. They had to take a boat ride out to it because of the water that surrounded the castle after a flood.

They then drove the Camaro 110 miles an hour across the *Bonneville Salt Flats* – 30,000 acres along I-80 near the Utah-Nevada border.

Before going across the Speedway, Emma decided to stock up on water and filled a quart-size leather pouch. Water was normally free, but a valued commodity at the flats and she had to pay two dollars for the fill-up.

Their tenth day was spent driving to Salina, Kansas, where they stayed in a *Ramada Inn* and had two meals, two drinks and two desserts for $3.94.

"It was the cheapest meal we've ever had. I still have the receipt! And it was good!"

Their eleventh day was spent in Louisville, Kentucky where they visited with his brother Billy, Jan and their two boys, Barry and Michael. Billy was stationed at the Fort Knox Army Base. They also visited the *Bullion Depository*.

By now, Nick and Emma were both getting tired of travelling and headed toward Huntington, West Virginia for the final lap home. They took a detour to Milton, West Virginia so Emma could visit the *Blenko Glass Company*.

Emma swore she would "never ride that far in a car again." And she hasn't to this day.

First vacation at Busch Gardens in Florida.

Nick at Los Angeles Coliseum

Emma getting water before going across Bonneville Salt Flats

Mary Washington Hospital, circa 1970's, where Emma worked in Labor and Delivery for 35 years. Picture Postcard from John Wayne Edwards

James Monroe High School, where Nick coached for 18 years. Original painting by John Wayne Edwards

PAUL'S DONUTS

Jack Glancy was another father figure to Nick. He and his wife Betty lived near Dahlgren in King George county. They had three sons – Paul, John and Richard – and two daughters, Mary Therese and Catherine.

Emma and John were the same age and graduated from high school together. John also played football against Nick. He was killed in an auto accident after graduation.

Paul Glancy served in the Navy for three years during the Vietnam War. He came home and managed *Scotty's Bakery* for a short period before deciding he wanted his own shop.

In 1973, Jack and Betty Glancy moved to Fredericksburg and encouraged Paul to follow his dreams. Supported him and his wife, Sandra, in opening *Paul's Bakery* which has become a popular tourist attraction next to *Carl's Frozen Custard* and *Allman's Bar-B-Q.*

Nick became friends with Paul and like Lloyd Gibson, would stop by the bakery in the mornings, spend an hour visiting with Paul. He often pulled out the donut holes while catching up on the gossip.

Nick knew the bakery donated day-old donuts to the homeless shelter and he would often take donuts with him to the fields when he coached the kids.

Jack and Betty Glancy treated Nick and Emma like family.

"Betty was so nice," Emma commented. "I don't think she ever met anyone she didn't love."

The Glancy's took Nick and Emma to Pittsburg to see a Baltimore Colts game at the *Three Rivers Stadium*, home of the Pittsburg Steelers.

"We rode in the *Duquesne Incline* cable car and got to see Pittsburgh at night. We stayed in a hotel and Betty's father 'the General McNeil' took us all out for a steak dinner," Nick reminisced.

The Glancy's also helped Nick and Emma prepare and file their taxes, aided when times were tight. They were like doting grandparents to Michelle.

Emma fondly remembers the time Mr. Glancy played Santa Claus with Michelle. "She was five years old and never guessed it was him. She sat on his knee, and he asked if she was a good girl." Emma chuckled, "I thought it was great that she really believed he was Santa Claus."

Jack Glancy encouraged Nick and Emma to open their own grocery store and took them riding to look at sites in Caroline and Spotsylvania counties.

"He said he would back us financially, but Emma and I were both hesitant. We aren't risk takers even though Mr. Glancy kept saying he believed in me and was always ready to go the extra mile for him. Up until he passed away, he would ask, 'are you ready yet?'

“That was another of those missed opportunities that might have made Emma’s and my life so different. I might not have gone into coaching.”

VOLUNTEER COACH

Lloyd Gibson left Caroline county in 1969 to become Head Coach for James Monroe High School in Fredericksburg. He coached track, football and basketball and served as the athletic director from 1970 – 1992.

"Coach Gibson was like a father figure to me. He kept me on the straight path so when he went to James Monroe and said he needed an assistant coach, I followed him."

Nick didn't have the educational qualifications but enjoyed working with the kids and volunteered as assistant coach at James Monroe until 1980.

He still worked nights at Grand Union but would train the kids at the high school in the afternoons before clocking in.

A worker bee, Nick converted an oversized storage closet into a weight room and located equipment where the kids could warm up or build their strength.

This small exercise room eventually led to a separate much larger training space at James Monroe.

"The kids were like sponges and I started off each season with my little speech. I'd make a fist with my hand, act like I was watering it and gradually open my hand up. Then I'd say, you are like this flower. Water it every day and watch it grow. When we get to the district, region or state, you will be in full bloom.

"Other times, I'd cup one of my hands together and act like I was watering it with the other. I would gradually open the hand as if the plant was growing. I'd say this is where you start, this is where you end. We're going to take it one day at a time. At the end of the season, I'm going to district, region, then state. Who wants to go with me?"

"I worked with some pretty amazing kids." Not everyone was a winner but just about everybody excelled to some extent."

Nick's face beams whenever he talks about athletes he has coached.

"Ray Greaser was my first rising star. When he started as a freshman, he threw the shot put 39 feet and the discus 110 feet. By his senior year, he was throwing the shot 58'6" and discus 164'4". Both became James Monroe school records at that time.

"Ray was one of those amazing kids that set all kinds of school records but never won the district."

Susan Glover went to the Stafford schools. She and her father, A.C. Glover worked to build her strength with the discus. Nick also helped to hone her skills and threw with her behind Grafton Village Elementary School. Susan went to UVA and was state and national champ in the Discus. She still holds the 1978 Stafford school record of 145 feet for discus.

"Four years in a row I had district champions – Jorge Leonarkis, David Williams, Kelvin Pearce and Mark Shepherd."

In 1976, Jorge Leonarkis threw 155 feet to win in a Spotsy invitational meet. Later in the season, on a rainy day, he placed fourth in the state.

The next year, David Williams won the district when he threw 153'6" and finished fourth in state.

When Kelvin Pierce competed in 1978, he always placed behind Martin Sparks, another thrower on the team. After some training with Nick, Kelvin, the number two thrower, beat Martin, the number one thrower and won the district.

"Mark Shepherd was another jewel." He won the district when he was a sophomore and threw the discus 158 feet. As a junior, he threw three times and fouled all three times, failing to qualify for the state competition. He came back in his senior year and placed third in the state with shot put at 50 feet and the discus at 157'6."

During this time, Jimmy Blanton was coaching at Caroline High School and asked Nick to work with Michael Lindsay, one of his throwers who had thrown the shot put 47-feet in the district and region.

Nick met with Michael on a Monday afternoon with a 22-pound shot put and a 16-pound shot put so he could see how they would feel. After Nick worked with him several days, Michael eventually broke Nick's 51'6½" school record at Caroline when he threw 52'7".

"Michael had never thrown over 50-feet in practice but on the first day I worked with him, Monday, he threw a 12-pound shot over 50-feet. Wednesday, he threw three over 51-feet in practice. We went to the state meet at JMU and he threw five out of six throws over 50-feet. His best was the 52'7" which beat my record."

Malcolm Taylor was a sprinter at James Monroe who credits Nick and Paul Neal at James Monroe and Ronnie Gosper at Stafford with helping him gain the kind of high school exposure required to land a track scholarship.

"I remember as a sophomore looking up at the record board and deciding I wanted to get my name up there. High school track was new and exciting for me. I discovered talents I never knew I had. My 9.6 was the fastest in the area but when I went to college, everybody was doing that."

Still, he says the discipline and training methods helped him in the outside world. (*Free Lance-Star*, Kurt Nicoll, May 14, 1988).

In 1980, Joe Ochertree lured Nick away from James Monroe and invited him to assist at Stafford High School. The school system was expanding and 1981, North Stafford High School opened.

Mary Bertolasio and Mike Rice started at Stafford as freshmen and trained under Nick. When they moved to the North Stafford campus, Nick continued to work with them on the side and they quickly became the best boy-girl combination in the weight events in one school. No one had done this since Susan Glover and David Saunders were at Stafford High School in the 1970's.

Mike and Mary worked with Nick any chance they could and since North Stafford didn't have a weight coach, they often shared what Nick taught them with their teammates.

"Our philosophy is coach now, throw later,' says Rice. 'It takes a lot of time, but it's worth it when someone starts to come around." (Kurt Nicoll. *Free Lance-Star*, April 12, 1983).

By the time Mary and Mike graduated from North Stafford, they had established the records for discus and shot put. Mary Bertolasio threw 38 feet in shot and 110 feet in discus; Mike Rice threw the shot 55 feet and discus 156 feet.

In 1983, the Spotsylvania coach brought Ray Barnett to Nick. He was a big guy – 6'4", 245 pounds. Nick challenged Ray in the shot-put ring just to see what he could do.

"Ray was leaning down, his head tucked to his chest as he prepared to throw the shot put. I pat him under the chin to raise his head for better balance and when I finally saw his face, Ray was smiling. I knew then Ray would go somewhere. I liked his attitude."

Ray was also on the wrestling team at Spotsylvania where the coach encouraged sneaky moves to win the competitions. Nick believed in competing honestly and told Ray he was a better man, encouraged him to quit wrestling. Which he did.

After the Stafford relays, Nick continued to work with Ray on the side with the shot put and the discus in their back yard.

"Ray ended up throwing the discus 180 feet and shot 60' 8" To my knowledge, the discus record is still there."

After he graduated, Ray threw in the Summer Junior Olympics in Seattle, Washington. At the nationals, he finished third in the Shot and third in the Discus. He wanted Nick to go with him, but Nick couldn't get off work.

"Ray was the best high school discus thrower I ever coached."

In 1984, Bill Micks, the Stafford wrestling coach asked Nick to put together a weight program for the wrestling team.

"That wrestling group was so dedicated to my program, they came on Wednesday nights to work out after their competitions.

"That was a proud moment for me when I realized how dedicated they were to fitness."

Mark Lenzi was also on the Stafford wrestling team.

"He was in the 132-pound weight class and held the school record in take downs. I worked with him and in two months' time, Mark's bench press went from 160 pounds to 240 pounds."

His junior year, Mark commuted to northern Virginia for diving classes and decided he wanted to give up wrestling for diving. After observing Mark at the RSL Summer League and at various pools, Nick knew this was a good decision.

"He was so amazing as a diver."

Mark Lenzi went on win a gold medal in the 1992 Olympic Games and a bronze in 1996 for diving.

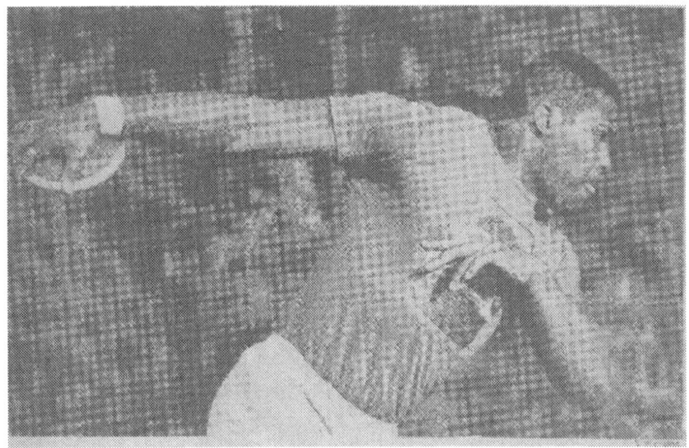

Ray Barnett. Photo from Free Lance-Star

BABIES AND MORE BABIES

Any time the moon was full, or the barometric pressure dropped causing thunder or snowstorms, Emma could count on a busy night in Labor and Delivery.

Being so close to Quantico, Mary Washington Hospital was the most central location for military family births. Sometimes she would start her shift with one or two patients and end up with eight or nine before it was over.

Some of the doctors would stay at the hospital during deliveries but most went home, leaving the nurses to track the mothers' progress and keep them posted. This was before fetal monitors and epidurals. Often, they would use "twilight" IV's to help mothers cope until the baby was ready to be born.

Emma watched them wheel the young girl into the room. She couldn't have been more than fifteen years old. She came up via the ER where she'd been admitted for stomach pains and had no idea she was pregnant.

This girl was no doubt the youngest mother Emma had worked with and she was ready to deliver any second.

"Throw it out the window," the girl shouted after the baby was born, "I don't want it."

Emma's heart stopped as she took several abbreviated gasps and looked up in shock when she heard the words.

She wanted a baby so badly. She and Nick had only been married a little over a year but were seriously trying to start a family.

She looked at Hazel Thomas, the other nurse on duty through eyes swimming with tears.

At the first opportunity, Emma raced to the staff bathroom, leaned against the door and wept. How could anyone say that about a small innocent baby?

"It was so heartbreaking," Emma sobbed with Nick hours later. He had come home to find her sniffling with puffy eyes and trembling chin.

"Hazel just shook her head, wrapped the baby in the blanket and handed it to the nursery nurses."

Little did Emma know, but weeks later, Hazel Thomas adopted the baby.

"The adoption process wasn't as difficult at that time and all the mother had to do was sign the baby over."

After years of using preventive measures, Emma wanted to relax, let nature take its course and start a family. She had already been charting her cycles but when nothing happened, she expressed her concerns with Dr. Lloyd who sent her to Charlottesville and Richmond for tests.

Twice she experienced the joy of success then the heartbreak of miscarriages – one at eight weeks and the second at ten weeks.

After five years of tests and disappointment, Emma decided to just forget about it for a while. Nick was thirty, she was twenty-nine, she accepted that maybe it wasn't meant to be.

Meanwhile, Emma continued to help women deliver healthy babies. She always knew what they needed whether it was a soothing voice, warm hand to grip, cold wash cloth, even laughter.

"Childbirth is a woman's most difficult time and my goal was to make sure the mothers were comfortable and family members in the waiting room updated.

"There were many happy times. Once, a woman expecting triplets was brought in. She was from Caroline County and had one of the triplets before we could move her from the bed to the table in the delivery room. Because of the multiple births, the hospital's NICU – neonatal intensive care unit – pediatricians and nurses were there to assist. The mother had the other two almost as soon as we got her situated on the bed."

There were also life and death deliveries. Once, one of Emma's high school teachers was brought in hemorrhaging.

"The beds were full except for one in the back. When we got her settled, we realized she was going to need a C-section, so we had to quickly move her from the third floor to the second where they performed the surgeries. It was tense there for a while, but it ended well."

In 1974, Emma's father gave them some property on the farm, and they decided to build a split foyer house.

"Unfortunately, we had to move a hill just to build on the property and dig an expensive 380-foot artesian well. That water turned the clothes and shower stall yellow."

Much as they appreciated getting out of the small apartment, this made for a longer commute for Nick. He was working in Manassas and had a forty-three-mile commute between the coaching at James Monroe and night work at the Grand Union.

With Nick working nights and her working days, Emma often felt they were ships passing in the night.

On September 19, 1976, Nick and Emma planned to have some quality time together and attended a Colts football game in Baltimore, Maryland. They were playing the Cincinnati Bengals and Roger Carr, the Colt's star wide receiver and Nick's favorite player scored two of the four touchdowns in their 28-27 win. Nick managed to get a signed and dated football that night.

On top of the world, they stopped at a restaurant in Waldorf for a steak and lobster dinner and couple drinks.

They were still driving the Camaro and took a little detour in King George on the way home. Nick drove down a long dusty trail, pulled over and parked.

It was a nice cool evening and the moon was full. Drinks relaxed them, his favorite team had won, the world was right. Perfect night for some lovemaking on the hood of the car.

AUNT ZOLA

Emma stepped out of the nurses' bathroom and her head jerked up when she heard a voice call out to her.

"Emma. Emma"

She gasped, felt the nausea return. Normally patients pushed the call button but for some reason this patient called out to her.

Emma experienced a blast from the past, it sounded so familiar. Her heart pounded and she experienced an urgent need to run down the hall.

"Emma," Laura asked as she approached from the opposite end of the hall, "are you okay."

Emma's face was white, her fingers covered her mouth, her eyes glowed brightly through tears.

"Aunt Zola," Emma whispered, "I heard her voice. She needs me."

Emma stood frozen in place, her thoughts all fuzzy and confused. Aunt Zola died seven years ago, she thought to herself. How could she be calling out to me now?

"It's a patient," Laura pat Emma's arm. "I'll take care of it. You go to the Lounge; I'll check on her, see what she wants."

Emma slowly made her way to the breakroom, collapsed in a chair.

Minutes later, Laura joined her. "Kathy's going to cover for us." She sat beside Emma, reached for her hand. "Are you okay? Can you tell me what happened?"

"I heard Zola calling out to me."

"Who's Zola?"

"My aunt," Emma shut her eyes as memories flooded her thoughts. "She died seven years ago. Here, in fact. At Mary Washington Hospital."

"But why would your aunt be calling out to you now?"

"I don't know," Emma whispered. "It was so out of the blue. She was my mother's sister; and like a second mother to me. I was so upset when she died."

"What happened?"

Emma swallowed, tried to collect herself. "Aunt Zola had polio when she was a young girl. She had to use the iron lung. She also had one leg that was longer than the other. She never married and supported herself by running the Goby post office in King George. She had a big old desk in a room off the side of her house where she sorted mail and people came to pick it up. She worked the post office, eight to four every day."

Emma smiled. "Zola was a smart lady. She had one of those old Singer sewing machines and my junior year, I had to make a dress from feed sacks for home economics. Zola didn't need a pattern; she'd made clothes all her life. She lay the material on that big post office desk, taught me all about the bias, how to cut the pattern, then sew it. She could have made the dress in one day, but she wanted to teach me. She still did a lot of the work, helped me pass the class.

"She lived over the hill from us and I could run back and forth between houses. During the snow season, someone would have to stay with her to put kindling in the wood stove to get the fire going and you know, warm the room. I sometimes spent the night with her and would get it going before leaving to go to school.

"One January night, I remember I didn't really want to stay that night. I think I had something at school and wanted to get some rest. I remember standing outside, waiting for the bus. It was cold. It was so quiet and peaceful. There was a dusting of snow on the ground. Suddenly I heard a voice calling, 'help, help' and I knew it was Aunt Zola. I threw my books inside the house and hollered to my mother that Aunt Zola needed help. I ran over the hill and my mother called nine-one-one and then drove over."

Emma paused, took a deep breath.

"Zola was putting the stove ashes outside and had fallen off the back steps." A tear escaped down her cheek. "She'd been laying there, I'm not sure how long. We didn't want to move her – her leg was broken – but we needed to get her in from the cold. The rescue squad arrived about ten, fifteen minutes later, and brought her here to the ER.

"They ended up admitting her to the hospital, but by then, it was too late. She was losing control of her body and developed pneumonia.

"I stayed with her here. For two days. I remember if I left the room and went up the hall, I could hear her calling out for me. 'Emma, Emma' and I would run back down the hall to her. That went on for several days. Aunt Zola passed shortly after that." Emma sighed. "We lost a good lady that January twenty-seventh."

"Is that why you decided to become a nurse?" Laura asked.

"Partly. But I really became a nurse because of my dad and was already taking nursing classes." Emma explained her father's heart attack.

Emma's cousin Eleanor, Aunt Zola and her mother.

When Emma was still nauseated the following day, she decided to go to the doctor. Make sure everything was okay.

Dr. Stoker came into the room and smiled. "I have some news for you," he said. "You're pregnant."

Emma was dumbfounded, just stared at him. After all the false hopes, she and Nick had pretty much decided maybe they weren't meant to have children.

"How many weeks?" She asked.

"We'll have to do a blood test, but I'd say four to six weeks. Right now, though, I'm more concerned about you. You've already had two miscarriages and working in labor and delivery isn't the easiest. I think you need to take some time for yourself and your baby. I'm recommending you stay off your feet a couple months."

As soon as Nick came home, Emma greeted him with the news. He was nervous. In shock.

Emma added, "On top of that, he's laid me off for a couple months and you're going to have to work harder."

They were living in King George and much as Emma liked living near her family farm, Nick's night schedule at Grand Union and her day hours at the hospital, made for long, tiring days. When Emma started having difficulties with the pregnancy, they realized they needed to move closer to town.

One Sunday afternoon, they took a drive to Fredericksburg to look for a new home.

They considered some townhouses and noticed a small house that looked like it might be the office. Nick talked to Francis Yeager, the builder who said the house wasn't an office and was also for sale for five thousand dollars less than the townhouses.

Nick and Emma decided the house offered more privacy and couldn't resist the deal – more room for five thousand dollars less.

They have lived on Southgate Avenue for over forty years.

Nine months after the Colts Bengal's game, and the full moon, Michelle was born.

Emma often asked if Nick wanted another child. A boy? He said he was happy having a healthy girl. He coached enough boys.

MICHELLE NICHOLS

Michelle Nicole Nichols was born on June 13, 1977, in Mary Washington Hospital at 10:37 PM

She weighed seven pounds, one and one half ounces and was twenty-two inches long. The delivery took six hours.

"It was amazing being on that side of Labor and Delivery," Emma recalls. "We had just started using the external fetal monitoring and I was dilating pretty good. Suddenly, Michelle's heartrate went down and I was fully dilated."

Emma laughed. "I had an epidural and requested one certain anesthesiologist because I knew he would give me more.

"By the time they moved me to the delivery room, the fetal heartrate had started back up and when I got to the room, all the nurses I worked with were standing around waiting with Dr. Stoker for the delivery.

Vonzi Pitts helped with the delivery and after Michelle was delivered, Vonzi started pounding on Michelle's feet to make her take her first breath. There was some tension in the room as Michelle needed to be on the oxygen machine to start breathing on her own.

"Michelle's feet were black and blue because of the cord being wrapped around her feet but Dr. Painter, her pediatrician said all was okay."

Nick was allowed in the room and commented afterwards, "if more fathers were in the delivery room, it might stop people from having six and eight kids."

Michelle Nichols has led an active life since the moment she took her first breath.

When she was two months old, Emma had problems with her gall bladder and was in Mary Washington's One East for several days. Michelle spent that time with Laura Hatch, Emma's best friend and fellow nursing partner.

When Emma developed jaundice, the doctors discovered she had gall stones and ended up removing her gall bladder.

Nick and Emma had scheduled their second trip to Hawaii for August but because of the surgery it had to be postponed and they travelled during the Thanksgiving holiday.

Nick laughed. "Michelle was five months old and we have a picture of her with her red hair in a solid blue suit with white pampers. I thought she looked patriotic."

Michelle has always been interested in sports and she started with swimming. Emma called her "water baby" because by the time Michelle was two years old, her swimming instructor had taught her how to swim under water.

Nick and Emma had a membership at the Spotswood Pool, and one afternoon when she was five years old,

Michelle decided she wanted to try out for the *Sea Serpents* swim team. She came out of the water, panting and crying but stated she wanted to be on the team. Soon, she was swimming year-round.

When she was eight years old, she swam for three different teams – the Rays, Year Rounds/US Swim League and summer league with the Spotswood Sea Serpents.

She became a mentor for other swimmers at the age of twelve and was a lifeguard from the age of sixteen until she graduated from high school.

Michelle attended Fredericksburg Christian School for grades one through five, then Walker Grant for her sixth and seventh grades, and James Monroe for grades eight through twelve.

Getting her to and from school was sometimes difficult. Depending on Emma's schedule, one of them took her to school, then Nick would pick her up and take her with him to the track while he coached until Emma got off work.

When she was five, Nick was coaching at Stafford High School and Michelle started throwing the discus. Her first throw was five feet – "I remember, she threw as far as her age" – and she continued to improve with practice. She enjoyed track and field and competed in the 100-meter sprint.

In 1987, she made her competitive start at the age of ten and placed third in the regional bantam girls (ten and under) shot put competition. She threw 17 feet-8 inches, making her eligible to go to the National Junior Olympics track and field meet at Brigham Young University in Provo, Utah.

There, she threw the six-pound shot put 18 feet-9 inches to finish thirteenth in the girls' division.

In the eighth grade, Michelle started throwing with the James Monroe team.

She always had a natural love for sports and watched football and basketball on television with Nick. She balanced track and field with other sports and in addition to her swimming, she played forward in field hockey for four years.

She was also a cheerleader for the basketball team for two years.

Michelle never liked lifting weights. She was too much of a girl and didn't want to build up her muscles. "I was more focused on being lean and toned than building muscle."

She was grateful for the regimented structure of sports. "It kept me organized in school. Whenever I was in my study hall, I always wanted to get my homework done so I could practice. I always strived to do my best and would be extremely disappointed if I received a B or lower in college."

Michelle doesn't remember a time when she wasn't travelling to meets, Scottish games or colleges. She visited over 51 colleges between swimming and track and field.

She earned twelve Varsity letters – four in Track & Field, four in Field Hockey, two in Cheerleading and two in Swimming.

She held the James Monroe High School Record in Discus at 129'11" for 20 years and was the Battlefield District Champion her Senior year in Shot Put.

In her career, she won Rappahannock Relays, Wolverine Relays, Caroline Relays, and Stafford Relays in Discus.

In 1991, she finished 5th in the USA Nationals and 4th in the AAA Nationals at Florida State and in 1995 was named James Monroe High School Female Athlete of the Year.

She was MVP in track for three years; and swimming for two years.

In swimming, she established records in 100 Free Style, 50 Free Style, and 100 Backstroke.

Michelle attended more track and invitational meets than any other thrower in James Monroe's school history.

She was first winner of the Mike Roadcap Memorial Award for track and field as well as the Emory Turner Memorial Track Award for track and field.

In June 2012, Michelle was inducted into the Hall of Fame at James Monroe High School, exactly four months after she had her first child, Olivia.

She graduated from Christopher Newport University and attended Kennesaw State University for graduate work, where she is currently working on her master's in criminal justice. She currently resides in Georgia with her husband, Sheridan, and two children Olivia and Kamren.

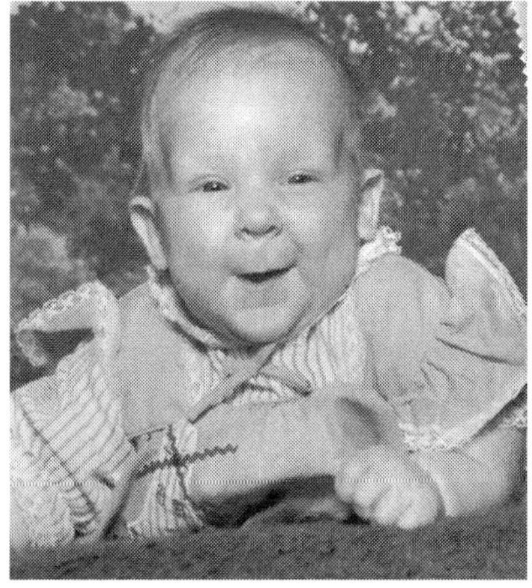

Michelle at six months

Michelle at one year

Michelle swimming at Spotswood Pool, Nick observing with his diet coke in hand.

Sea Serpents

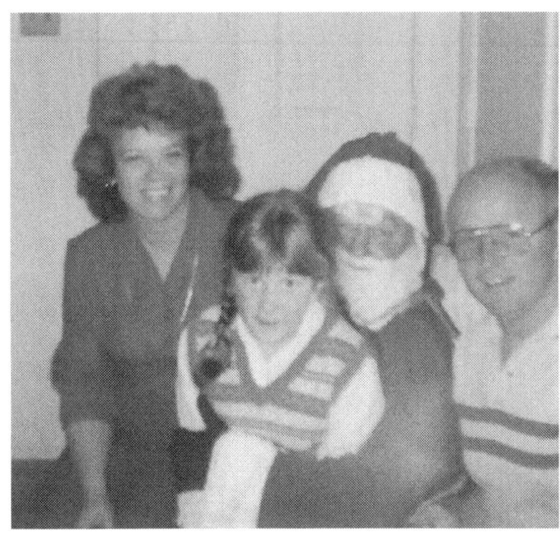

Emma, 5-year old Michelle, Jack Glancy and Nick

Gymnastics with the Gymnastics Magic Saints

Michelle and Nick after she broke the James Monroe record with the discus throw of 129'll" in 1995. Photo from Free Lance-Star.

Second place at AA state meet at James Madison University.

Cheerleading for two years.

Field Hockey for four years.

Discus meet at age 14.

State shot meet, finished fifth with 36'5"

Shot put at James Madison University State Meet

HIGHLAND GAMES

The roots of the Highland Games date back to the 1300's in Scotland. They were introduced in the U.S. in the 1850's at Boston, Massachusetts, and are held nationwide during the summer months. Men wear kilts and bagpipes provide music.

Strength is a requisite; technique, speed and coordination help. Events include: 56-pound weight toss for height; 56-pound and 28-pound throws for distance; 22-pound blacksmith's hammer throw; 17-pound stone put throw; sheaf toss (competitor uses pitchforks to toss bags of straw over raised bars) and caber toss (competitor balances and tosses large sixteen to twenty-foot tapered poles).

Shortly after Michelle was born, Nick read an article in the *Washington Post* about the games. It featured Ed McComas, a fuel company executive from Baltimore, Maryland who had been competing professionally since the games became popular on the east coast in the early '70's.

They were holding a competition for professionals and amateurs at Alexandria Episcopal High School in Alexandria, Virginia and Nick decided to give it a try.

To prepare himself, he began throwing 12-pound hammers, cinder blocks and large stones – anything that came close to the necessary weight – behind the house.

At his first competition, Nick participated in the amateur division and won the stone throw.

A few years later, Brian Oldfield, another professional who lived on the West Coast competed in a game where Nick once again competed as an amateur. When Nick won the stone throw Dave McKenzie, one of the competition organizers, decided to let Nick compete with the pros in the stone throw, that event only.

Brian Oldfield held the American indoor record at 75 feet, but at that competition, Brian only threw the stone 53 feet. Nick threw 41 feet.

Nick could never imagine throwing that close to a professional and carried the article about his competition against Brian Oldfield in his wallet for many years.

He didn't wear the kilt until his fifth year and competed until close to his fiftieth birthday. "When I first started the games, there was no animosity. Everyone had fun." Then things changed, it was more cut-throat and he lost interest.

Emma always enjoyed going to the Highland Games in Roanoke, Norfolk and Williamsburg, Virginia and Idlewild Park in Ligonier, Pennsylvania. Many of the competitions were held near the mountains which provided a nice backdrop. She sometimes felt like she was in Scotland.

One of her favorites was the Norfolk games at the Botanical Gardens. "I met a full-fledged Scotsman who told me so much of the history of Scotland and Ireland."

Nick at shot put competition.

Nick practicing in his back yard for a Highland stone toss competition with his 43-pound pet rock. Photo by John Paraskevas, Free Lance-Star

CARL BRAUN

Nick watched Carl Braun walk across the field. He was 6'3" and 215 pounds of muscle. He was on the basketball team but pretty much kept the bench warm, scoring a total of four points during the two years he played.

Basketball season was over, and the track coach said they needed a thrower. Nick figured Carl was the perfect candidate.

"I know you played basketball," he told the boy, "but you're built to throw."

Nick handed Carl the discus, took a few minutes to show him how to handle it. "Now, I want you to throw this. You'll probably throw seventy to ninety feet but let's see what you can do."

Carl tossed as hard as he could and when they checked, it was seventy-five feet.

Nick grinned. "See, I told you. Now," he handed him the discus again, "I want you to do it again."

By the end of the afternoon, Carl was throwing almost ninety feet.

On their way to the locker room, Nick tossed out his challenge.

"Robbie Gilmartin is throwing 140-feet, but we need another thrower to combine with his distances to win the Stafford relays. I think you're the man. Our first meet is middle of May."

Carl stopped in his tracks; his jaw dropped as he stared at Nick, wondered if he heard him correctly. "It's April first. You're telling me by May fifteenth, six weeks from now, I'm going to be good enough to compete?"

Nick's lips twitched. "With my help. We'll work every afternoon," he rested a hand on Carl's shoulder, "but you can do it. Now," he hesitated, looked Carl in the eye, "are you ready?"

Nick and Carl worked every afternoon in preparation for the meets. Carl appreciated that Nick always challenged him to do his best, but he knew it drove his mother crazy. Every afternoon he could see her waiting patiently for practice to end. But before Carl could leave, Nick would tell him to throw the discus *one more time* past a target.

"Until you pass that point, you can't go."

Soon, it was time to face the competition and Carl found himself competing against Spotsylvania's Ray Barnett.

"Ray's good," Nick warned, "I've worked with him, but you're just as good. Just give it your best shot."

Carl accepted the challenge and consistently finished first or second.

In the district, he threw 134 feet and placed 4th. Then he threw 137 feet and was 5th in region.

While they trained, Nick kept talking to Carl about throwing the javelin. He knew a coach from Tennessee who was looking for a javelin thrower he could work with from scratch and make a national champion.

"I don't even know what a javelin is," Carl complained. All he knew was it was some sort of sphere.

But Nick kept saying "you can throw it. In fact, I predict you can throw the javelin 200 feet and finish in the top 10 in the nation."

Nick gave the Tennessee coach Carl's phone number but he never followed up with either of them.

Carl had already sent in his letter of intent to go to Longwood College, but Nick thought he would receive better training at Christopher Newport. Their coach was also looking for a javelin thrower. He introduced Carl to Vince Brown who invited Carl to come to Newport News one weekend to tour the school and compete in an open meet.

"How'd you do?" Nick asked when Carl returned to school the following Monday.

Carl smiled. "I cleaned up. They invited me to come back so guess what? I'm going. Just cancelled my Longwood letter of intent and start there this fall."

After the relays in June, Nick worked with Carl throughout the summer, preparing him for a career with the discus at Christopher Newport.

Nick had been competing in the Highland games for seven years and felt Carl would be a good candidate.

"Don't they wear kilts? And throw telephone poles?" Carl asked, then laughed. "YOU put on a woman's skirt?"

"And toss a telephone pole," Nick rebutted. "You should try it. I'm doing a competition in Williamsburg this weekend. Why don't you come with Emma and me?"

Carl attended the games, thought it was cool watching professionals throwing hammers and spears, flipping 20-foot telephone poles. And wearing kilts.

~~~~~~~~

Carl Braun graduated from Stafford High School in 1984 with Marc Lenzi and Jeff Rouse – "three guys from one school that had goals" and achieved spectacular success.

Carl attended Christopher Newport University and trained briefly under Barry White his freshman year. Scott Black became his coach in his sophomore year and reinforced everything Nick taught him. He became proficient with the javelin and placed tenth in the nation his senior year. Just as Nick had predicted.

"Pretty awesome for a little guy from Fredericksburg, Virginia," Carl likes to say.

Carl followed Nick into the Highland Games, bragged how he could do anything.

"I had spent some time in the weight room and had a pretty successful freshman year at Christopher Newport I figured I'd give it a try.

"So, I go out to one of the games and Nick is the ultimate coach. He's smiling and bragging, 'This is my man.' He introduced me to all these guys, but my hardest challenge was wearing a kilt. I kept thinking *I'm not wearing a skirt. I'm going hold out as long as I can.*

"Then I saw this big guy. I mean, he's huge. He's six foot three, weights over 360 pounds and has no neck. And he has a kilt on." Carl shakes his head. "I decided if he can wear one, I can.
~~~~~~~~

"I competed and was third overall winner. Nick was fourth or fifth. Then when they were doing the recognition, it hit me. I had beat my coach. That's every athlete's dream.

"The summer of my senior year, '88, I turned pro, went back to the games in Williamsburg for my first competition. And I won it which was amazing."

From 1988 to 1994, Carl competed professionally. He travelled to Scotland five times and set records. In 1994, he was the #1 athlete in the world.

Carl became a three-time national champion and third in the world. He also set several American records.

"What Nick was able to do in a short amount of time was give me the self-confidence to do the impossible. All of this was through positive thinking and the heart of a man who saw potential, believed in me and harnessed my strength. That's the real blessing.

"I've always considered myself the little guy from Fredericksburg who had a coach with a big heart. He has a God given gift to see potential in people. A skill many people don't have. He taught me how to compete, to do it right and stand up against the best athletes in the world."

From Nick ~ "Carl is one of my most incredible stories – that you can read your athletes and say they can do something they can do. All I tried to do was put him on the right track, converted him from a basketball player to a weight thrower.

"He could throw anything. I think he could throw a refrigerator. His family brought the Scottish games to Fredericksburg and for two years, they were held at Maury Stadium."

Carl Braun, age 23. Photograph by Tommy Price, staff photographer, Free Lance-Star.

Carl Braun preparing to do caber toss

NICKEL GYM

In 1986, Bill Libby needed a throw coach at Courtland High School. Bill also offered a small stipend making this Nick's first paying coaching job.

When Nick received his first coaching paycheck, he made a momentous decision. He had coached for fifteen years for free – ten at James Monroe High School and five at Stafford High School.

"I want to give back to the community," he told Emma. "I want to open a house gym for the kids. Keep them off the streets."

"You're running on fumes now," Emma stated, "Where are you going to find the time to do this gym?"

Emma never questioned supporting his idea, just wondered how and where they were going to get the equipment.

She, Nick and nine-year old Michelle started cleaning the small attached garage on their house.

"I talked to Dale Taylor about some of his equipment. When he realized what I want to do, he sold me a set of 400-pound Olympic Weights, a bench, squat rack and a curl bar for $300.00."

"It was the best investment I ever made," Nick recalled years later. "That's how we got the Nickel Gym up and running."

The gym was open three days each week – Mondays, Wednesdays and Fridays – from three to six in the afternoons, fifty-two weeks each year.

"We needed some rules," Nick stated, "we couldn't just let anyone walk in.

"First, the kids had to be between the ages of thirteen and eighteen, and I had to meet their parents. I told the kids flat out, if your parents don't care about you, I don't care about you. This is my house and here are the rules to the gym. There would be no smoking, no drinking, no cursing, no drugs, no earrings and no tattoos. If you don't like it, don't come.

"We also told the parents if they wanted to sit and watch their kids, they could do so. If they wanted to work out with their kids, they could work out. If they wanted to call to check on the kids, they could call. If they saw anything they didn't like, they could take their kid out of my house.

"The door was never locked. There was no reason for me or Emma to be locked up with their teenager. We weren't going to be accused of anything."

It was a blessing that Emma was a nurse and always in the house. They were fortunate that they never had any real need for medical assistance.

There were no fights because another rule was if two people fought, those same two people left.

Nick's motivation was to give something back to the community and allowed the kids to use the gym free of charge although some families made small donations.

The average number of kids using the gym was twelve although at times, there were as few as two or as many as twenty-four in the fourteen by twelve room.

Some stayed a little past six o'clock, but Nick said to be sure to turn the radio off and lock up before they left.

Nick designed a "pyramid" regimen for everyone where the kids increased their weights five pounds each week.

Monday was max day; Wednesday was light rep day and Friday was heavy rep day. If you missed either one of your lifts that week you had to stay at that weight until the next week before you could move up to the next five pounds.

Nickel Gym ~ 3-6 PM

Monday – Max Day – pyramid up and back down
(key lift) is (MAX)

Wednesday – Light Rep Day – 3 sets of 10 reps
(key lift) (3 sets of 10 reps)

Friday – Heavy Rep Day – 3 sets of 3 reps
(key lift) (3 sets of 3 reps)

After six months, when the gym was being readily used, Nick set a donation jar in the corner.

"I told the kids, if anyone wanted to contribute, it was a five-dollar a month donation or nothing; we treat them both the same. If you've got the money, I'll accept the donation. I can't be bothered with who paid and who didn't. I wanted to give every kid an opportunity to work out."

That jar helped Nick and Emma to reward the kids for their hard work. They also used the money to buy more equipment – a curl bar, weights, squats, stationary bike, sit-up bench whatever they could get in the room.

They decided to do a *lifter of the month* recognition and Jim Teter, who owned a sports shop, designed a 5x7 plaque. He sold them to Nick at half price. He also engraved the kids' names on little brass plates so their names could be added to the yearly plaque that hung on the wall. Jim's two sons also lifted at the gym.

The money in the jar paid for the plaques. To be eligible, the kids had to increase their bench press ten pounds during the month. If two people tied, they gave two plaques.

Then everybody wanted t-shirts, so they decided to do *Nickle Gym* shirts. *Graphic Designs* sold them the shirts at cost, and Nick and Emma sold them for seven dollars each. The money from the sales of the t-shirts went back into the jar.

The last five years they started giving trophies and Nick reached out to Mike Loving at *MVP Sports*. He had coached Mike at James Monroe. Mike gave them a discount and helped when they started giving bigger trophies.

Every Christmas Nick and Emma hosted an Award's Ceremony in their fourteen hundred square foot house. One year, there were 43 kids and parents in attendance from three to six that evening.

"The house was packed. They were on the couch, chairs, wrapped around in the dining area, down the hall. Everything was full. It was a good evening though. I stood in front of my retirement chair and gave out the awards.

"Money from the donation jar paid for some of the food but the hard part was Emma would have to do the cooking. She'd fix lasagna, shrimp, meatballs, casseroles all kinds foods. Sometimes people brought salads, tacos. It was a lot of work, but it made for a fun evening.

"There were rules for the Awards night too. From three to six we catered to the young people; between five and six we cleaned up then at six, the adults came. The adults could drink beer but not while the kids were there. I had a cooler of beer, if they wanted something, fine. I don't drink any more. That's another story."

The Nickel Gym also worked with two kids with special needs.

Mike Canady was autistic and started working in the gym his sophomore year of high school. He had problems controlling his breathing while lifting the weights, so Nick decided to begin at the basics and started Mike on the twenty-pound bar. Mike was benching ninety-five pounds when his father came in and stated he could do more than that.

"Let me handle it," Nick answered. "We always add five pounds each week."

Mike ended up benching 410 pounds and went on to participate in a Special Olympics and the Open Division.

Nick also helped Mike with his writing skills. "I'm a common-sense guy," Nick always said. "keep up your education, you can learn new things."

Mike had to write out his workouts.

Landry Hefler was legally blind. He'd been shot in his right eye with BB gun and had a glass eye. Nick knew he could barely see and was worried when Landry's mother said he wanted to come to the Gym. Unsure of how well he would do, Nick offered to work with him one Sunday to determine his abilities.

"I got him to lay on the bench to check his technique with the bench press and with his limited vision. He started at 160 pounds and progressed to 280 pounds which was good for him.

"He wanted to learn to throw the discus and because of his left eye being his good eye, he could compete with the discus and won the Spotsylvania meet even though he was legally blind.

"I would say we worked with 200-250 kids during that twenty-year period. Many were high school students. but we also worked with college students from University of Mary Washington.

Alex came with his girlfriend. "He had a tattoo on his wrist, and I said he needed to cover it up. I explained I had a rule and couldn't have him influencing my young people."

Alex agreed to cover it up.

"That's the kind of people we worked with. Everybody worked together, cared about each other. The older kids always helped the younger ones."

The Nickel Gym impacted many lives. Jean Williams discovered the gym through her daughter, Faith Shortal.

Jean was an RN scheduled for knee replacement surgery on both knees and was looking for a recovery program. She bench-pressed to strengthen her upper body strength for getting in and out of chairs.

"She was an independent lady and made her rehab much shorter because of her training."

She worked out three times each week for fourteen weeks before the surgery and maintained the weightlifting after the surgery to keep active.

At first, she was nervous because the room was filled with lifters in their teens and twenties. She worked beside Emma who was bench-pressing two-hundred pounds. She also used the treadmill and all the exercise not only boosted her energy, but it also made her more confident about defending herself.

She was named *Lifter of the Month*, May 1997 and was most proud of that accomplishment.

"Weightlifting helped keep her independent spirit alive," Emma said.

Brian Musselman weighed 155 pounds and did a 300-pound bench press. He lived in the neighborhood and would come near closing time and stay later. He worked out with loud music and would lock up when he left.

He earned his name, "muscle man" went on to work on the police force at Mary Washington University.

Nick also worked with three kids at Courtland that broke track and field school records. John Walsh threw the shot put; Mike Digarmo and Derek Pletch were right and left handed discus throwers.

In the first meet, Mike threw the discus 149' and broke the school record. The day before that, Nick had put Derek in the ring at practice and critiqued his throws – picked him apart. After practice, Derek went to Nick, his uniform in his hands and said he felt like he knew nothing about the discus and was quitting.

Nick felt bad, and called Derek's mother that evening, offered to work with Derek if he would give him an hour a day.

"Derek was an average discus thrower, only throwing 120-130 feet, but after I worked with him, he threw 141' for 6th in the district. We went to the regional and he threw 144'. We went to the state in Williamsburg and he did even better – 158'6" for 3rd place. The winner was Ray Barnett.

One Friday evening at 4:30 PM, Nick was trying to rep 390 pounds. Micky Tingler and two others were spotting for me.

Nick was pushing up and his elbow snapped. Everyone heard it. Nick's arm went straight down, and the spotters kept the weight from landing on his chest. Micky caught the weight and the other two helped put it back on the rack.

Jean Williams was also there, and helped Nick into a chair in the kitchen.

Emma looked at the clock, saw that it was 4:45 PM but reluctantly called Dr. Marriott Johnson's office.

"We're fifteen minutes away and have an emergency," she stammered. "Can Dr. Johnson see my husband before he leaves the office today?"

They went to the office where they x-rayed Nick elbow, found it was a torn tendon.

Dr. Johnson had worked with football athletes before and knew he would be on call that weekend. He said he would do the surgery the following morning at 7:00 AM.

Nick and Emma had made a date to go to the movies that Friday night and much to Emma's surprise, he kept his date. Nick went to the movie theater with an ice pack and pillow under his elbow.

The following morning, Nick had the surgery and Dr. Johnson said he probably wouldn't lift over one hundred pounds again.

Nick had nine weeks of recovery and nine weeks in rehab. His first day back in the Nickel Gym was a Friday. He tried to bench press the bar which weighed 45-pounds and couldn't do it.

Saturday morning, he was cutting grass and pushed the mower ahead of him as hard as he could. He kept doing that over the entire yard.

The following Monday was *max* day in the gym, and he decided to give it another try. He started with the 45-pound weight and lifted it ten times with no problem. Jean Williams was also there and he looked at her with the biggest smile on his face.

He started increasing the pounds and gradually worked his way back to 350 pounds.

"I also realized I had been lucky and maybe it was time for me to hang up the weights; spend more time with my wife.

Three women bench-pressed over 200 pounds during the history of the gym – Emma (215), Megan Tingler (215) and Lamir (210).

Five guys benched over 400 pounds – Derek Sears (410), Mickey Canady (410), Nick (415) Keith sellers (420) and Micky Tingler (465).

Jean Williams.
Photo by Davis Turner,
Free Lance-Star

Mike Degarmo spotting for John Reck.

Some of the kids from the Nickel Gym.

Nick and Gold medal Olympic Champion Jeff Rouse

Nickel Gym team, minus Mike Canady that went to weight-lifting competitions at Fitness Zone.

Megan Tingler, Emma and Micky Tingler in Nickel Gym.

WEIGHTLIFTERS:
I would like to thank each and every one of you for all of your hard work and dedication at making yourselves Bigger, Better, and Stronger. You have grown Mentally as well as Physically. Thanks to you, the Nickel Gym Works. I'm very proud of each and every one of you!

Keep Pumping!

Someone who cares,
Nick Nichols

Plaque to inspire Nickel Gym lifters.

Nickel Gym money jar. A plain jar that funded equipment, trophies and awards ceremonies. Still has money in it!

LeCRESA WILCOX

In the spring of 1987, the year after Nick opened the Nickel Gym, Emory Turner, track and field coach from James Monroe said, "Nick, it's time for you to come home to James Monroe."

Nick coached at James Monroe until Michelle graduated in 1995.

The first thing out of the ordinary Nick noticed was he had four boys, no girls to coach.

"I'll get you some girls," Emory stated and the next day, LeCresa Wilcox and Tasha Goudy showed up for practice. One week later, Tammy Coghill joined the team.

Nick arrived and found them sitting on the ground beside the bench.

"First thing," he said, "there is no sitting down during practice. If you see me sitting down, you sit."

The girls looked at one another then stood.

LeCresa had never been involved with track and field and in fourteen months, established herself as top female shot putter in Fredericksburg.

During practice, she threw ten-pound shot puts which were heavier than the ones used in competition.

In her first meet, LeCresa threw the shot put 29 feet which tied the girls' record at that time. She threw the discus 69 feet. Her second year, she threw 43' 11" in the shot put and the discus 120'11".

In the regional meet at N.C. State University she placed third in both the young women's shot put with 36'6" and the discus, 111'3".

In the Summer, she qualified to compete in the National Junior Olympics at Brigham Young University in Provo, UT.

Each athlete had to raise approximately $400 in local sponsorships to cover expenses.

Nick went to all the businesses in Fredericksburg for those sponsorships to Utah. Managed to raise all the money needed for the plane ticket, hotel stay, room and board, food.

"You did it by yourself," she cried when he handed her the plane tickets.

Nick admitted later that he almost had a nervous breakdown when he had trouble making the flight arrangements for everyone. This was the same Junior Olympics that Michelle attended for her first time. He had worked all night and was functioning on very little sleep.

LeCresa placed 11th in the shot-put competition with 38'9" and 15th in the discus throw with 112'5".

"Not bad for her first season," Nick bragged. "In three to four months she finished in the top six in the region to make the nationals."

On Saturday, April 30, 1988, the 3rd Annual Battleground Invitational was held at Mary Washington College. It was an eleven-hour meet with 46 boys' teams, 43 girls' teams and thirteen records. There were long waits between events and coaches and athletes worried about tightening muscles.

Nick was there with LeCresa and had her start slow during warm-ups.

LeCresa had a 40'4" throw in the girls shot put preliminaries, then threw 41'11" in the finals, breaking the meet record of 41'6." She also won the 4th place in the girls' discus.

LeCresa held that shot record for twenty-eight years until it was broken in 2016.

After graduation, she competed a second time in the National Junior Olympics in Gainesville, Florida and placed 5th in the shot put – 40' 7"

"Le Le was a hard worker. She has a big heart and loved to throw. When she was having a hard day, she always came back. When she was backed up against the wall, she came out fighting.

"Her key to success was dinner, a good night's rest and preparing mentally. Always saying, 'I want to do this'."

~~~~~~~~~~

"I was sixteen years old when Nick started working with me. From the word go, he and Emma always been great to me. They were always in my corner, treated me like family. They were my surrogate parents. I was Michelle's big sister.

"Track and field has been Nick's passion and he kept pushing us to be the better person. He took me to competitions all over – places I'd never been to before. I
~~~~~~~~~~

accomplished a lot through him. He was always encouraging me to do my best.

"I went to their Nickel Gym and spent a lot of time at their house. Nick and Emma didn't treat me any better than their own. They went to the end of the earth for us kids."

LeCresa also enjoys dancing and often went with Nick and Emma whenever she could. She even taught them to do the electric slide. "Right in their living room," she laughs.

She also watched and cheered them when they were on the television show.

LeCresa Wilcox after winning at the Junior Olympics. Photo from the Free Lance-Star.

Throwing shot at James Madison University meet, 1988. Photo from Free Lance-Star.

Micky Tingler

Micky Tingler followed his brother Lee, up the short sidewalk to the small one-story house on Southgate Avenue. His first thought was it didn't look like a gym.

Their father, Pepper Tingler, grew up with Nick in Caroline and was Nick's insurance agent. When Nick explained his plans for the Nickel gym, Pepper decided this might be something that would benefit his kids. Micky was a sophomore, Lee a senior and both played football at Caroline High School. They also had a younger sister, Megan.

Micky knocked on the front door and a balding white-headed gentleman with a big smile came to the door. Not the biggest guy in the world, Micky thought. He most definitely didn't look like a weightlifter.

Am I in the right place? Micky wondered.

Nick led the boys around the corner of the house to the side entrance to the Gym and gave them a tour of the small room. Micky had dabbled with weightlifting but not seriously.

The first thing he saw was the sign on the wall – *Rome wasn't built in a day, be patient.*

"It's all about technique," Nick explained. "We're going to start with the very basics and develop a good base. Like a pyramid – the higher you go the sharper your skill."

They started with an easy, doable workout schedule modifying it from time to time.

"It made sense in a lot of ways to see some consistency," Micky explained. "Nick had a way of looking out for you. You would make some progress, but not wear yourself out."

All the lessons started and just kept going. Nick would write workouts for everybody based on their skill.

There were never any conduct issues. No fights. "We all knew the gym was their home and we needed to behave."

Paul's Donuts would often be provided and everyone wanted to get there early to get some.

"They were giving out trophies by the time I started going there and everybody had to work to certain levels to be eligible. Conduct, outside of the gym was important as well. Nick and Emma had a way knowing how we did in school. It was mostly young people competing for the trophy and we wanted to win that thing."

Micky's younger sister, Megan played hockey at Caroline, but she enjoyed dance as well and didn't want to be too pumped up physically. Nick's personality made it fun for her and she learned to drive a hockey ball a lot farther. She bench-pressed 65 pounds and grew to 215 pounds.

Lee eventually went off to college but every Monday, Wednesday and Friday, Micky and Megan travelled to Fredericksburg to work out in the Nickel Gym. They scheduled doctors' appointments and holidays, even after-school jobs in the city around their lifting workouts.

Fortunately, they didn't have to be there precisely at three and as long as Nick had time he was there.

"He worked night shifts in addition to his coaching, often functioning off four hours sleep. They were determined to be there and open and did that for twenty years. There were times when they might have been out of town. Megan and I oversaw the gym when Nick and Emma were away.

"I started working in some restaurants in high school and I usually worked Thursday through Sunday. Friday was nice. I would work out, take shower at their house, change and Emma would have a plate of dinner waiting for me before I went to work. Sometimes I stayed up there."

Both Micky and Megan attended weight-lifting competitions with Nick and Emma, representing Nickel Gym and accumulated many plaques and trophies.

"Working out at the gym improved our focus in school, added dedication in our athletic endeavors and established a camaraderie over time. Everybody knew one another."

Micky started bench pressing at 215 pounds and grew to 465 pounds. He also did three sets of ten reps at 335 pounds.

"Nick could see subtle things to make you do better. He was good at taking people to that next level. People wanted to be there and experience Nick's passion that led to success.

"Most coaches are about themselves, Nick was all about the kids.

"Emma is the strong silent type. She was a little opposite from him, quieter, but she was always there. I never asked for any dinner, but she made sure it was there. Nick does all the talking and Emma's the team mom and keeps him focused.

"I like live music and when I was old enough, I started going out dancing with them." Micky laughs, "everybody thought I was their son."

"Nick and Emma are my friends. Like second parents to me. My perspective is probably a little more than others. Emma would sometimes go visit with Michelle and I would visit with Nick. He's not a loner, prefers being around people. I did that more than once. We never went to clubs or dances when it was just us."

Micky shakes his head. "Whenever they had those Christmas parties, they would have 30-40 people in their small house. People would be all over, just hanging out. We would have potluck dinners but Emma also prepared a lot of the food. Her lasagna was delicious and always the first to disappear."

In 2000, Micky, Megan, Mike Canaday, Jean Williams, Lemiur Eillis, Nick and Emma competed in local gyms and oftentimes placed first overall as a team.

Micky appreciated that Nick operated the gym for twenty years for the local students. "He considered it his community service to keep the kids off the streets. Everyone was treated the same whether they contributed to the donation jar or not. The money was used to purchase plaques and trophies for monthly and annual recognition of lifters.

"Emma has been a perfect, steady match for him. She reigns him in while at the same time doesn't smother him. He's successful because of her. There's a partnership there. They are there for each other.

"The first thing I think of when I see them is they are a happy dedicated couple. Good match. Great people. They have had a significant impact on a lot of people.

"Together, they have found a way to do a whole lot with not a lot. Hardworking people - nurse and stocker. They've done a whole lot in their lives by being thrifty, smart and doing the right things."

Micky with his Nickel Gym Lifter of the Year trophy which he won two years in a row.

Micky's sister, Megan, won the Female Lifter of the Year trophy two years.

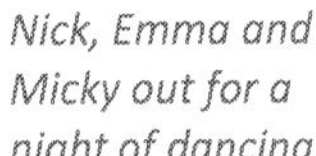

Nick, Emma and Micky out for a night of dancing.

A NEW MARY WASHINGTON HOSPITAL

Laura Hatch started working at Mary Washington Hospital five years after Emma. In the early days, they averaged 75 deliveries a month. By 2009, they were averaging 200-275 deliveries a month.

Emma was the first person to detail Laura to labor and delivery procedures.

"From then on, we had each other's backs, depended on each other. We developed a strong sisterly bond that is still steadfast today."

They learned how to work with the different doctors, understood their different, sometimes quirky, procedures of delivery and C-section surgeries.

The doctors were there for the delivery and to make rounds but it was the nurses that took care of the patients, saw to their comfort and kept the families informed during delivery.

Laura laughs. "Whenever a new doctor would come on, we'd have to teach them the ropes."

The doctors didn't always stay at the hospital during delivery, most lived nearby and had to come from home.

Once, a patient went to the bathroom and was further along than they knew. She came out of the bathroom, hollered and started pushing.

Carol, one of the nurses on duty, was with the patient but when the baby started crowning, Carol had to act fast.

Labor and delivery nurses are taught to protect the baby's head which Carol did, but by the time Emma and Laura arrived to help, Carol was pale as a ghost.

In 1993, change came to Mary Washington Hospital. They moved to a new location, organization adjusted and technology began to impact procedures.

In the old hospital, departments such as labor and delivery, nursery, surgery, etc. were on separate floors or wings and everyone worked together within their unit. In the new hospital, everything was in one unit.

In the old hospital, Emma, Laura, doctors and nurses wrote everything on paper. In the new hospital, computers changed the documentation process, Internet opened a new world of sharing that information.

First, they had to transfer all their patients to the new facility. They tried to pick a day that wasn't busy, discharged whomever they could, then moved the others one by one.

Computers and continuing education became a necessary part of the new workplace. Not only did Emma and Laura have care for the patients' needs, but they had to learn how to use a mouse, remember program procedures and navigate a keyboard.

In the old days, they might have to travel to Richmond or Charlottesville whenever a patient was transferred. Now, they were travelling for computer training. Oftentimes, to come back and teach to other nurses.

Through it all, Emma, Laura, Peggy, Dixie and Sandra worked side by side, helping doctors deliver babies, assisting with C-sections, even putting salt in an anesthesiologist's coffee machine for fun.

They often celebrated birthdays, kids' weddings and Christmas together. Some even went dancing with Nick and Emma.

Laura was Emma's rock during every celebration and crisis.

"Emma and Nick are two of the best people on earth. Emma is like my sister and I can't be more blessed than that. They are two wonderful people who will do anything for you. An outgoing, fun-loving couple. Nick always jokes around a lot. Hugs me longer than anybody else."

In 2005, Emma nominated Laura for Nurse of the Year and presented her with the plaque at a special recognition ceremony.

MARY WASHINGTON COLLEGE

In 1996, Nick was still nights at Grand Union in Alexandria, Virginia, and Stan Soper offered him a coaching job at Mary Washington College. "I'm just a high school coach," he thought. "What do I know."

Nick didn't take the offer but decided, "if he offers me the job next year, I'll take it."

Stan offered it again, and Nick stayed there for ten years, until 2006.

Nick did no recruiting. "Whoever came out, I coached. I'm not Einstein or anything great."

He considered himself a "molder of clay" and always looked at the finished product at the end of the season.

"Once again, I started with my little spiel. I'd close my hand, pretend to water it. You have your flower, water it every day and watch it grow. That's how I coached."

The young people he worked with were like sponges, in full bloom at the track meets. They absorbed his challenges. He always said it's not how you start but how you finish. Let's get started.

"Men's records were set in shot put, discus, hammer and javelin. Women's records were set in all the events except javelin.

"Indoor track records were set in 20-pound weight throw for women and 35-pound weight throw for men."

While at Mary Washington Stan Soper was named Coach of the Year in Men's competition, 2000-2003 and Women's competition, 1998-2005.

The school was named Team Champion in the Men's competition, 1997, 2000-2003 and Women's competition, 1997-2006.

"In 1996, I also coached two high school girls on the side – Kelly Gordon and Melissa Messick. Kelly set the high school record of 120' with the discus that hasn't been broken yet. She went to William and Mary."

Notable women's athletes at Mary Washington were Michelle Kelly who was the first to break the discus record in 1997 with 114'9", Jamie Smith who was rookie of the conference in 1998 and Candy Bush who did well at the conference with shot and hammer in 2001.

Carissa Culbreath worked hard, studied hard and held two records – 43'3" with the 20-pound weight in 2005 and 135'4" with the discus in 2006.

In 1997, Hilario Ellis won the Conference in the discus with 124'7" and Bob Shelton won the Conference in the hammer with 148'8".

Mike Privett was a leftie that broke the discus record with 154' and the hammer record with 148'11" in 2000.

Tyler Vose was from Montana and threw the javelin 192'5" in 2001.

Jared Bankos was from Cherry Hill, New Jersey and won the 2003 Conference with his 160'5" javelin throw.

Jason Istvan came out of nowhere and won the hammer in the 2006 conference with 135'1". He broke that the next year with 140'3".

Tom Swigart broke the shot record at 48' 3"in 2009.

"We had some outstanding athletes in conferences and throws. Those were a fun ten years."

1999 – "what a year"

Where sports were concerned, 1999 was a good year. Nick was coaching at Mary Washington College at the time and the Nickel Gym was going strong.

"We had people from all over the area in our little gym."

One was Samantha Hall from Stafford. Nick started working with her when she was a sophomore, helped her throw the discus from 110 feet to 135 feet. Samantha came to the weight room, built up her skills then the coach took over and took all the credit.

Her senior year, she was working out in the Nickel gym and Nick struck up a conversation.

"Do you need me to work with you? If not, I'm gonna get somebody to beat you." He joked.

Nick was also working with three guys in three different schools – Carl Banks from Stafford, Amir Ramanpur from Courtland, and Jason Cherry from Chancellor.

Early in the outdoor season, Carl Banks had the best throw of 153 feet in the discus.

Amir Ramanpur was left-handed Iranian throwing the discus 120 feet. I would watch him and offer suggestions, but his coach wasn't happy about my helping him. Nick invited Amir to the gym and started throwing the discus once or twice a week after hours at Spotswood Elementary School and in the back yard.

"I told Amir, Banks would be coming down in discus and he would be going up, peaking."

At the District meet Amir threw 147 feet and Banks threw 133 feet.

At that District meet, Nick watched Jason Cherry from Chancellor. He was a 6' 5" 230-pound sophomore. He threw 125 feet for fifth place.

I went up to his coach and asked why Jason wasn't spinning during his throw and the coach answered he'd been trying to break the habit but he didn't seem to understand."

Nick worked with Jason on Mondays and Wednesdays for several weeks at Chancellor High School with a round rubber tire.

At the regional meet, Banks placed second with 143 feet; Amir was third with 142 feet; and Jason was fourth with 140' 11".

The next week all the boys practiced for the state and the weekend before the meet, Nick met with Jason and his parents in the living room of their house.

"We're going to let them know about Jason Cherry this weekend," Nick stated.

They went to State meet at Norfolk State and on his second throw Jason threw past the school record of 148 feet with 158 feet and finished 5th in the state.

Carl Banks threw 150 feet for sixth place and Amir threw 147 feet for tenth.

Nick beamed.

"Three guys from three different schools and all three placed in the top 10 in the state. That is crazy."

JAMES EBERHARDT

James Eberhardt was twenty-four years old and had served in the Air Force for six years. He was a good thrower in high school in York, PA and practiced with Olympic Champion, John Godina at UCLA.

He also had a daughter who lived in Virginia with her mother and decided to take advantage of the GI bill to better his life. He wanted to get it done quickly and still be near his daughter. He reached out to several Virginia schools – one being the University of Mary Washington – and had settled on Virginia Tech. The scholarship was locked in and all he had to do was compete in one meet.

Then Mary Washington's head coach, Stan Soper, called him. "Why don't you come out to the Battleground Relays this weekend, check it out."

James was hesitant at first but decided to check it out.

When Stan Soper walked James down to the throwing area and introduced him to Nick, Nick asked, "What's the Virginia Tech shirt for? You're going to come to Mary Wash."

James laughed. "I'm just here to see the meet, I've already decided on Tech."

"Okay," Nick persisted, "how long can you stay?"

"I've got a few minutes."

Nick introduced James to the Mary Washington athletes as well as those on the other teams. James was immediately impressed by the friendly, relaxed comradery among the teams.

Nick handed James a discus. "Why don't you give it a try?"

As the day progressed, James watched Nick help kids from all the schools, reminded everyone about respectful behavior, even demonstrated a few dance moves.

"When will you be at practice?" Nick asked, when the entire team regrouped at the end of the event.

Nick looked at James' *Virginia Tech* shirt and said, "you won't be needing that shirt. It's a done deal." He offered his hand. "Welcome to the team."

James smiled, decided he liked this guy. Liked his personality. "I need to fill out an application first," James challenged.

"Let's go find Coach Soper." Nick turned, marched off.

The following Tuesday, James took his application to Stan Soper and on Thursday, he received a call from the admissions office. James later admitted, "that's when one of the best decisions in my life was made."

The next week, Nick called James. "I'm going to be out on the track training, want to come? Watch me do a workout."

James agreed and they spent four hours together.

"He brought a box of *Paul's Donuts,* I'd never heard of the bakery. And a 12-pack of diet drinks. I learned that anytime you saw Nick, he had a Diet drink in his hand.

"We had a fantastic time. It was one of those moments where you meet someone, and you seem comfortable. We talked about all kinds of things – family, staying on the right path. There was nothing off with Nick.

"We were throwing the discus and he kept telling me to throw it a certain way to follow through and pull it in bounds. I couldn't do it and kept throwing it out of bounds. He kept telling me to try it again and I just couldn't get it.

"I was frustrated. He was frustrated. And I was getting angry.

"Finally, Nick picked up the discus and looked at me. He said, 'you're not going to listen to me. I'm not going to help you.' Then he threw the discus behind him.

"I looked back and all I could think was I was going to have to go get it.

"But Nick said, 'now, let's take a walk.' He wanted me to calm down. Nick has a special way of working with young people."

James thought it was ironic that his first indoor track meet was at Virginia Tech, the school he had turned down. During the meet, Nick kept telling him to throw the shot a certain way, but James got stubborn and threw it his way.

James stepped too far, fell to the ground and sprained his ankle.

Nick and Emma drove home in the middle of the night from Blacksburg, Virginia, and took James to the Veterans' Hospital ER in Richmond to have his ankle examined.

"They sat with me at the hospital. I'd been hurt in high school but never had this attention before."

The doctor told James his season was over since there were only three weeks left of indoor track, and he couldn't expect to be back in shape.

Fortunately, the school was starting fall break, so James spent the first week in Physical Therapy and practically lived in the training center, kept putting ice on his ankle. By the fourth week, he was back.

"We had nine Battleground meets and I won them all. But my proudest moment was when Nick said, 'you're what I thought you were made of'."

His sophomore year, James slipped during a meet at Liberty University and broke a finger.

"But I placed second and third in two events. I also came close to making nationals."

His junior year, James made the nationals for the first time. Nick worked with him during the summer, invited James to train two days a week in the Nickle Gym.

After a series of eliminations of other participants, James qualified for the nationals again during his senior year and went to Wartburg College in Waverly, Iowa with Stan Soper and Nick for the division three national championship.

"They only take the top fourteen in the nation and I got in by inches."

The night before, they were eating at a *Steak and Shake* and Nick said, "James, we're where we want to be. You know the ones that care about you are with you."

There were no distractions and Nick's last words to James before he went onto the field were "I'm proud of you."

James walked onto the field, saw the train going by on the railroad tracks in the distance and thought of his father.

Then he thought of Nick and realized he wanted to give Nick, and Stan Soper, a good show for all they had done for him.

He threw and knew he did well but had no idea how well as he wasn't familiar with the metric system of measurements. His second throw was even better, but he still didn't know how much.

That second throw measured 179'9" putting James in fourth place in the nation.

Nick watched from the stands and when James threw his second throw, he jumped up and shouted, "YES! That's my man! James Eberhardt from University of Mary Washington. My man did what he was supposed to do. I don't care what the rest of you throw today, we got what we came for."

After the event, Nick grabbed James' cell phone and called Emma who happened to be walking around the Mary Washington track at the time.

"Emma," Nick shouted excitedly, his voice cracking, happy tears flowing down his cheeks. "I'm okay. Nobody believed in James. He threw 179.9! He's fourth in the nation. I'm so happy I don't know what to do."

James graduated from University of Mary Washington in 2005, returned in 2006 for his master's.

He continued to participate on the team and once again qualified for the nationals. He attended Benedictine College in Lisle, Illinois for the division three national championship but due to problems with the injured ankle he threw 166 feet.

He also didn't get as long to warm up because he and another thrower were talking in gym and didn't hear the announcement for their flight. They were late coming out missed the warm-up time.

James was the Capital Athletic Conference winner for the discus in 2003 (159'2"), 2005 (157'9") and 2006 (166'4"); and the shot put in 2005 (45'.25") and 2006 (46'2.5").

He was also named Mary Washington's Athlete of the Year in 2006.

"**N**ick has a special way of working with young people. He was my inspiration. I had the GI Bill and would take classes at night. Monday through Thursday, I would get off work, run on the track, drive home, go to night classes Monday through Thursday. Friday night was my only free night but then I had track on Saturdays. Many nights I was tired.

"Then I'd looked at Nick and realized his schedule wasn't any better. And he was still doing so much with the kids. I figured, if he's done it for thirty-five years, I can do it. It was good to have that inspiration.

"I appreciated what he did with the gym. Some of those kids were struggling with grades, being picked on. Nick found a way to bring them up – put his nickel on them – and the kids walked away feeling good. That's what Nick and Emma are about – service to others.

"Emma was the mother I never had. She cared about me, followed up with me, kept things organized. Had an open heart and was fully supportive.

"She was the team mom for the throwers, loved the environment and our success. Everything started and ended with her."

After college, James went dancing with them a few times. He also saw them when they were on television. "Nick likes the attention on the dance floor."

James and Nick at the competition at Wartburg College in Waverly, Iowa.

COLIN DWYER

Colin Dwyer attended Mary Washington College from 2000 to 2004. The college became a University in his senior year. He and his two brothers had gone to a Catholic school and his parents were very involved in their boys' lives.

"Colin wasn't a big guy – 6'1" 175-180 pounds," Nick says, "but he was fast. He had a good technique and lots of personality.

"His sophomore year he set a record in the 35-pound indoor hammer throw with a throw of 51' 3".

Colin was an avid fan of John Powell, a four-time member of the U.S. Olympic team who specialized in the discus. Powell did training camps and videos for young people to learn to throw the discus.

John Powell said, "there are two kinds of people in the world, those who believe they can and those who believe they can't. And they're both right."

After practice, Colin would go back to his dorm room and study the videos. Even his father said he studied them when he went home on weekends.

"Colin was always trying to do better," Nick says.

For indoor track, Colin threw the 35-pound weight 55 feet for a school record that hasn't been broken yet.

In outdoor, he threw the shot put, discus and hammer.

"He was first in the hammer throw in 2002 with 163'7". What was amazing though was he threw 7'7" further than the second-place winner."

Colin was the school's Rookie of the Year in 2001, Conference winner for the discus in 2002 and 2004 and went to the Nationals at St. Lawrence University, N.Y. in 2004 and finished 11th in the nation.

Colin shared a friendly rivalry with James Eberhardt during their school years and continues to keep in touch with James.

Nick, Emma and Colin shared a special bond outside track and field. His studies prevented him from working out in the Nickel Gym, but he often visited their home to chat or attend the Christmas parties.

Colin graduated in 2004, did two tours in Iraq then came back to the states.

"Pound for pound, Colin was the best complete thrower I had at Mary Washington."

Colin and Nick at University of Mary Washington. Photo from Free Lance-Star.

Colin, Emma and Nick.

James Eberhardt and Colin Dwyer

DANCE CONTESTS

In 2000, Nick and Emma were in North Caroline for a track meet for Mary Washington. Afterwards, they decided to stop by the *Durham Hilton* to dance. They strolled up to the door of the club and were greeted by two big bouncers.

"How much to get in?" Nick asked.

"Ten dollars."

Nick gave him a ten-dollar bill and waited.

"Each," the bouncer announced.

"For a DJ?" Nick exclaimed.

When they walked into the Club, they were greeted by two more bouncers – one shorter than the other.

Nick walked up to the shorter one and said, "Keep your eye on this old man."

When Nick and Emma stepped onto the floor and started dancing, many of the ladies in the room jumped up and joined them.

This became the norm whenever Nick and Emma visited the clubs.

Shannon's Lounge in Fredericksburg was one of their favorite night spots and when Nick read about their dance contest, he decided to enter. He and Emma won their first trophy. It was twelve inches high and proudly displayed on a shelf.

When Nick discovered they were hosting another contest the following week, Nick asked if he and Emma were eligible to enter a second time. The answer was yes, and they returned to win their second trophy which was a little taller – eighteen inches.

When *Shannon's* held another contest the next week, Nick asked again; they said yes. Emma was concerned they wouldn't win but Nick responded, "don't worry, just be yourself."

As luck would have it, this was the finale. Nick and Emma won, and the trophy was even taller. They never expected to win all three but had fun all the same.

In 2001, they went to *Gecko's Waterfront Cantina* in Woodbridge, Virginia. It was a Thursday night and they were there just to dance. The waitress mentioned they would be having a dance contest and the prize was $100.

"Let's give it a shot," Nick tempted Emma.

Participants were required to dance successively and as the contest progressed, the judges came around, encouraged them to continue – "hang in there, you're doing great."

Two songs later, Nick and Emma finished the contest and won the $100.

Feeling lucky, Nick began to search for other dance contests and discovered one close to home – at a night spot in the Westwood Shopping Center on Route Three in Fredericksburg.

This competition was based on the audience applause and the first time they participated they won the $100 prize.

They went back the next week and based on the applause, should have won but placed second instead.

Nick wasn't going to argue with the judges but decided to compete individually. He danced against the ladies and won $50.

Years later when they were visiting with Michelle in Atlanta, Georgia, they went to the popular *Opera Nightclub* where a DJ was entertaining the crowd. As soon as Nick and Emma started dancing, everyone began watching them and clapping.

The Manager offered to buy them a drink and invited them to the VIP section upstairs. When Nick and Emma arrived upstairs, the manager moved the tables and chairs from the front of the clear glass that overlooked the dance floor below. Nick and Emma were invited to dance in front of the glass. The crowd downstairs looked up and started clapping in rhythm to the music.

"It turned out to be a very memorable night. It was a really upscale club and the only time we went there."

The following New Year's Eve, they went to the *Vegas Nights* Dance Club in Marietta, Georgia. The interior looked like a theater with a stage on the lower level. Their seats were on the second floor.

"Shy me, I told Emma let's go up on the stage and dance."

Once again the crowd cheered them while they danced.

When they returned upstairs, Nick invited the DJ from one of the local radio stations to join them. She said she was working but would join them when she finished. That made for another memorable evening.

Nick and Emma's Dancing trophies.

HAWAII

Emma and Nick never had a real honeymoon and they always liked the warm environment, thought Hawaii would be the perfect place to vacation. They visited other tropics – Bermuda, Bahamas, Jamaica – but Hawaii is their favorite. So much so, they have gone back six times – every five years.

"We were poor folks, but I worked hard at the hospital and Nick worked hard at the Grand Union to save money for these warm vacations."

Nick always set up the trips and in 1973, the two of them flew to Hawaii for two weeks for $1400. Nick still has the receipts.

They try to go in August, close to their wedding anniversary. Fortunately, Hawaii isn't as crowded. "Many people tend to go there around Christmas."

Their first trip was also their first time on an airplane. Nick planned four stops so they would get used to going up and down. Holding hands, the entire way, they flew out of Washington, D.C., to Tulsa, OK, then to Oklahoma City, California and finally Hawaii.

"We never had any problems flying after that," Nick bragged.

Emma smiled. "Hawaii is where I met my tall dark and handsome guy. He was our tour guide." For several of the trips, Vern Brash took them on the tours; arranged for them to island hop with *Hawaiian Air.*

They went to Pearl Harbor and saw the *USS Arizona* Memorial on their first trip. Later trips included visits to the *Polynesian Culture Center,* Elvis Presley's mansion on the North Shore, a pineapple plantation and many other scenic sites.

"Over the years, we've watched the islands become more and more commercialized."

Waikiki Beach in Honolulu was their favorite island; next was Maui with the crystal blue water and waist-high waves. The Black Beaches, created by the lava from the volcanos flowing into the ocean, were also a favorite.

One day, Nick was swimming in Waikiki Beach and forgot he had $30 in his pocket. He looked down, saw his money floating on the water. Luckily, he retrieved all the bills before they drifted too far.

Several times they have joined others on the outrigger canoes. "It was so much fun, and fifteen dollars each! They helped us get the canoe in and out but the views and exercise were spectacular."

Nick started singing the song, *Tiny Bubbles*. "We saw Don Ho several times. He had a little club on one of the side streets near the hotel and would have his family at the shows. Michelle also saw him in '04." Don Ho passed away in 2007

Their last trip, in 2014, they saw Mavis Staples of the Staples Sisters in the Hawaii theater. "She was amazing," Emma exclaimed. "She was in her late seventies and still sang wonderfully. I guess people that have sung all their lives are used to it."

Nick and Emma couldn't dance at the concerts but haunted the nightclubs every evening. Wherever they went, people watched, appreciated their style.

Nick chuckled. "We went to this one nightclub; the band only knew a handful of songs and every third one would be Tony Orlando's *Tie a Yellow Ribbon*. They would take a break and as soon as they started again, someone would request the song."

In 2009, they were in Honolulu, near the *Ala Moana* shopping center for their 40th anniversary. They went into the *Rumors Nightclub* and started dancing.

The dance floor was packed. Nick noticed two life size cages on each side of the stage.

"You get in one," Nick stated, "I'll get in the other."

They started doing the same steps in the cages which brought cheers from the crowd. After a few dances, they stepped out and others began having fun in the cages.

In 2004, they went to *Aaron's Atop the Ala Moana* a restaurant on the thirty-sixth floor of the Ala Moana Hotel in Oahu Hawaii. The food was out of this world, the view of the Pacific spectacular.

Michelle had graduated from Christopher Newport University in 2000, and was with them for her college graduation present. She looked across the way, recognized Fantasia Barrino who had just won the 2004 American Idol contest. She also recognized Jennifer Hudson, a finalist in the same season.

Nick and Emma started dancing, figured they would get the two girls' attention. Sure enough, they worked their way over, started a conversation, got some autographs and posed for pictures.

When Nick and Emma started doing the electric slide, Jennifer joined them on the dance floor. A slow song came up and Nick started the dance with a dip to the floor.

"Wait a minute," Jennifer Hudson exclaimed as she ran to the table to get her camera. Nick managed to hold Emma in the dip until Jennifer could snap the picture.

Nick and Emma usually rented cars for their trips until their last visit, they struck up a conversation with a policewoman who not only recommended local places to eat but suggested taking the shuttle buses wherever they wanted to go. "She even found a schedule for us."

One day, a small tsunami hit the islands. Unaware of the weather forecast, Nick and Emma had taken the bus to see the Waimea Falls and then on to North Shore.

"I just wanted to see the Falls then go to the North Shore and get me feet wet,' Emma said. "I walked to the edge of the water, and one minute I was appreciating the warm water and the next I was flat on my back, staring at the sky.

"The undertow was so strong, it literally flipped me and started taking me out to the sea," she exclaimed. "There was coral in the water as well. Nick grabbed my hand, braced his feet in the sand and started pulling me out." Emma paused. "That was one scary, scary moment.

When they returned to the hotel, they realized there had been an alarm. People were no longer on the beaches and it was evident that the waves had crested much closer to the hotel.

Another scary weather-related incident was when they were caught in a hurricane in Freeport, Bahamas.

Nick shook his head. "There was no warning, but we knew something was wrong when hotel staff started taping up the windows and putting the chairs in the pools."

Nick and Emma had a flight out the next day but the hurricane hit that night.

"The windows were boarded up but with the force of the wind, water seeped around the edges of the plywood and soaked the carpet in the room. Power lines were down and there was no water."

Eastern Airlines planes had already left the islands ahead of the weather but returned the next day for their regular flights.

Emma's cancer relapse prevented their return to Hawaii in 2019 for their 50th anniversary but they hope to go back soon.

"If not, I've told Nick, when I'm gone, he can cremate me, take me back to Hawaii and scatter my ashes on the beaches."

First Plane ride to Hawaii

First trip to Hawaii

Michelle accompanied them on many of their trips.

Bermuda trip

Loving the beach and visiting Don Ho.

Visiting Aloha Stadium in the 50th state.

Beautiful scenery. Inspiration to return again and again!

Nick and Emma at the front of the team

Nick and Fantasia, 2004

Michelle, Jennifer Hudson and Emma, 2004

Emma, Nick, Fantasia and Michelle, 2004

CANCER

In 2002, Emma went for her yearly checkup.

"Gail was the technician that did the mammograms and I went to have my annual checkup. I routinely checked myself but never felt anything so you can imagine my shock when they found the cancer in my left breast. Luckily it was all encapsulated, they were able to remove it and I just had to have radiation."

Emma received daily radiation treatments for five weeks then fought an infection the sixth week. The treatments were tiring but not enough that she gave up dancing.

She and Nick still went dancing every Thursday night and Emma tried to maintain her strength in the Nickel Gym.

When they got the news that Emma was in the clear, Jean Williams had just finished working out in the gym and was standing by the telephone. She, Nick and Emma all hugged each other.

"Ladies," Nick said, "we got the good news today but someone else got the bad news."

"Every man sooner or later will have problems with prostrate," Nick said.

In 2010-11, Nick went for his annual checkup and learned he had an enlarged prostate. The primary care doctor sent him to a urology specialist for further tests.

It was discovered that Nick has an athletic heart – the result of his training in sports – meaning his pulse rate is very low.

The initial examination was too painful for Nick, so they decided to sedate him, and the anesthesiologist had difficulty maintaining his blood pressure.

When they determined it was prostate cancer, they thought it was encapsulated. Dr. Gregory Szlyk performed the robotic surgery. When he removed the prostate one of the cancer cells escaped. Nick undergoes the PSA tests every three to six months for monitoring purposes and continues to be cancer free.

In 2019, after seventeen positive yearly checkups, cancer returned to Emma's right breast. Again, she never felt anything, and worries about Michelle.

"I was shocked when I got the news. I kept asking why me? Why did I get this way?

"I was depressed. And angry. I snapped at people. I remember waking up one night and seeing a light in the corner of bedroom. I worried the Lord was going to take me but I kept thinking I wanted to stay. I wasn't ready to go.

"I believe in prayer. My mother taught me this and it brought back memories of Aunt Zola, I can't tell you enough how much the lyrics – He walks with me and talks with me – from *In the Garden* played through my mind."

After several tests, it was determined Emma's cancer was unique. Her, estrogen receptor was positive and the HER2 tests were negative, making Emma ineligible for pathology tests with the Mayo Clinic.

The single area of Ductal carcinoma in situ (DCIS) – a non-invasive or pre-invasive cancer – and the nuclear grade was two out of three. There was no evidence of invasive carcinoma with that AJ2A stage so they decided that she would have chemo. The first test was negative.

There was a lot of apprehension and time between tests for worry but Emma decided she didn't want to have a mastectomy. She decided she was going to fight it and chose both chemo and radiation.

For four months, Emma endured the treatments and never let it interfere with their love for dancing. In fact, the day after her first chemo treatment, she danced a short while at Steve Jarrell's show at the Fredericksburg Fair.

"I'd be sick a couple days after a treatment but then I'd be fine."

Nick was by her side for every treatment and Laura Hatch and many of her other nursing friends called or texted daily to check up on her.

"It was very humbling and sometimes, I think the Lord was talking to me. Once, I met a woman who was also a nurse and had worked in an adjoining office with me.

"Her name was Jennifer and she had three kids – two boys, sixteen and twelve and a six-year-old daughter that was full of personality. Jennifer was in her early forties and had been struggling with brain cancer for some time. She still homeschooled her children and substituted for vacationing nurses in the office. The day we met, she was at the office for test results.

"I realized that day how small my world was and how cancer was not selective regarding age, occupation or person. It was very humbling and almost brought me to my knees.

"I realized I had been blessed with a full life, loving husband and circle of friends that checked on me every day."

"Now we're waiting to get the good news again."

RETIREMENT & LIVING THE LIFE

In 2000, Nick gave up the commute to northern Virginia and retired from Safeway Stores, Inc. Used to being busy, he painted the house inside and out.

Six months later, he started working four twelve-hour days as a material handler – junk mail – in Fredericksburg.

After her first cancer scare, Emma retired from Mary Washington Hospital in 2002. She decided she wanted to spend more time with Nick.

They had a retirement party for her at the hospital and in 2003, Laura Hatch, Emma's best friend, hosted a surprise retirement party for Emma at Renato's in Fredericksburg.

They were still running the Nickel Gym and they began lifting weights together and competing with the Nickel Gym team.

They also spent more time on the dance floor on weekends. She also looked forward to travelling and spending time outside.

After a couple years, she wanted to "keep the brain going" and have more spending money. She decided to stay in the nursing field and worked part time in an OB/GYN office., so she work.

Nick closed the Nickel Gym in 2006 after injuring his elbow but continued to work in material handling until 2010 when he went to work for FedEx in Stafford County where he stayed until April 19, 2018.

Nick continued to compete in the Virginia Senior Games and in 2007, at the age of sixty, he threw the discus 151'1" at the University of Louisville, Kentucky, to finish 2nd in the nation. He retired from the games in 2012.

They returned to Hawaii in 2009 for their 40th Anniversary and started going to concerts at Busch Gardens – Kool & the Gang (2008), KC and the Sunshine Band (2013), American Idol Scott McCreery (2013) and The Tams (2015)

Nick smiles. "Little Red, with the Tams has invited to dance with them on stage four different times." Anytime they went, Nick always managed to be dressed in the same colors.

One Sunday afternoon, they were going to *Two Times New* at the Greenbrier Shopping Center and heard a woman singing. The doors to *Jay's Restaurant* were open so they followed the music and went inside.

There weren't very many people inside. When the woman stopped singing, Nick went up and complimented her. Asked who she was.

"I'm Sheila Ray Charles," she responded. "Ray Charles was my father."

"We stayed for the rest of her performance," Emma said.

They saw entertainers, Dr. Oz, Charlie Daniels and Kellie Pickler.

"I don't know what happened to me when I saw Kellie. I just froze for about a minute. I was so surprised, I couldn't move."

The avid Baltimore Colts fans, Nick and Emma saw Raymond Berry on November 16, 2011 at Randolph Macon College in Ashland. They also saw Johnny Unitas.

Emma's retirement party at Mary Washington Hospital. Photo from Free Lance-Star.

Nick dancing with The Tams.

Nick and Sheila Ray Charles.

Dr. Oz.

The Embers

Jim Quick and Coastline

Righteous Brothers, March 7, 2020.

Raymond Berry of Baltimore Colts

Johnny Unitas of Baltimore Colts.

Lenny Moore of Baltimore Colts

CHUBBY CHECKER

Chubby Checker has been Nick's favorite entertainer since his youth. He learned to dance with his music and has seen him perform six times. He has always been very polite and still singing today.

"Chubby used to come to Busch Gardens and in 2006, he had two shows, two years in a row. I danced the first show in shorts, went to the car and put on my dancing shoes, then went back for the second show.

"Chubby would invite people up on the stage with him. He must have a good memory, or thought my twisting was good because he always invited me up to the stage and saved me for last.

"He even autographed one of Emma's pictures, 'Emma, Nick's girl'."

In 2011, Nick and Emma travelled to Myrtle Beach to participate in one of Chubby's attempts to break the Guinness Book of World Record. They were trying to get as many people dancing the Twist in one spot at the same time.

All participants were given an *I Twisted with Chubby Checker in Myrtle Beach!* tee-shirt and he and the crowd of almost two thousand were supposed to dance in a designated area near the boardwalk for five minutes.

A Beach Music Festival was going on at the same time across the street and there was some confusion when Chubby accidentally set up on one of their stages. He had already started the set when officials realized the mistake. Moving the band equipment required a lot of manpower and time so Chubby continued to play where he was.

Nick had been waiting at the designated stage and when he heard Chubby playing across the street, he pushed his way through the crowd of almost two thousand to the other site. By the time he arrived, there were too many people around the steps to the stage. Nick held his hands up in the air begging to join them on the stage. Some in the crowd took pity on him and pushed him through the crowd toward the stairs on the side of the stage. Nick had one foot on the step when Chubby reached down and pulled him up onto the platform.

There were enough twisters in attendance to break the record but by the time the officials had reconciled the confusion, too many had left before the five minutes were up.

The next time Nick and Emma saw Chubby was when they visited Michelle and her family in Atlanta in 2012. Chubby was doing a *Sunday Family Day* at the Anderson Center in Marietta Georgia. Once again, Nick and Emma danced on stage with the twisting rock n' roll singer.

Nick's tee-shirt from the Guinness Book of Records effort in Myrtle Beach, South Carolina.

Emma dancing with Chubby.

Nick twisting with Chubby.

Michelle, Nick, Emma and Chubby Checker.

Emma, Chubby, Michelle and Sheridan James, Michelle's husband.

JULY 29, 2017

On July 29, 2017, Nick and Emma decided to attend a Ludacris concert at the Celebrate Virginia *After Hours* at Central Park, a popular shopping/event center in Fredericksburg.

Emma wasn't crazy about going as she wasn't too fond of his lyrics, but Nick persisted. "He's got the beat."

"You need tickets," the gatekeeper stated when they arrived at the entrance.

"How much," Emma asked.

"Thirty-five dollars."

"Each," Emma exclaimed. She shook her head, turned to Nick. "I'm not paying that much. We don't even like his songs."

"I'm here, I'm going," Nick argued.

The local DJ was warming the crowd with J-Kwon's song, "Tipsy" when Emma followed Nick onto the open field. She kept her eyes lowered, self-conscious of the looks as if everybody couldn't believe a couple their age would be at a concert like that.

"If we're going to do any dancing, we better do it now," Nick said as he boldly made his way toward an opening in the middle of the audience. He set up their seats and started dancing. Emma followed suit, noticed quickly that people began watching and smiling at them.

Jaimie Ashton and her husband were celebrating their anniversary at the Ludacris concert. They were already settled mid-way back, enjoying the pre-show music.

She watched Emma and Nick stroll past her and smiled, surprised that they would be interested in the Ludacris music but thought to each his own.

Minutes later, she heard laughing and cheering behind her and turned around to see the couple dancing, delighting in the beat.

But what melted Jaimie's heart was the lopsided grin Emma shared with Nick. She did that with her husband all the time.

"It was so refreshing just to see them enjoying the night together. And the crowd cheering them on."

Jaimie grabbed her cell phone and videoed the couple dancing side to side. She posted it on Facebook, simply to share the fun moment with her friends.

The concert started and Jaimie didn't immediately notice the number of her friends that liked, then shared the video.

"My couple friends turned into ten thousand in a couple hours! It was insane! My phone was going off all night. My kids were laughing at me, saying 'you're going to go viral.'"

Jaimie laughed. "I didn't even know what viral meant."

Her video was eventually viewed thirty million times with one hundred forty thousand shares in one week.

Suddenly the world became aware of Nick and Emma Nichols.

Jaimie had never met this couple and suddenly she was getting messages from people all over the world. People wanted to do blogs, magazine and newspaper articles, even radio interviews.

People commented on the shares, talked about how Nick was their coach, or Emma was so nice. "Everybody seemed to know them except me," Jaimie stated.

"No one realized what inspired me to do the video. This was right before the uprising in Charlottesville (Virginia). My family is bi-racial, and my heart was hurting from all the racial tension in the world. Seeing them enjoying the music and hearing the crowd cheering them on had a healing effect on me."

Jaimie had a friend that knew Michelle and put them in touch with one another. Jaimie and Michelle decided to create a Facebook page – *Nick and Emma The Dancers Page*.

Suddenly, Nick and Emma's faces and moves were appearing all over the world.

"If you haven't fallen in love with this viral dancing couple, you're about to," HOMEBT.COM, a news station in the United Kingdom stated before playing the video.

That story led to an article in an Irish paper later that day.

J-Kwon shared the video on his Facebook; David Muir with ABC World News shared the video in his broadcast; Buzzfeed, even InsideEdition.com played the video.

They were invited to do radio and television interviews and were the subject of several articles in the local newspaper – *The Free Lance-Star.*

Radio and news stations across the country were calling for interviews – Fredericksburg.com, FREDNETRADIO.COM and LIVE 99.3 (Fredericksburg), KHOU 11 (Houston, Texas), 11ALIVEE.COM and Fox 5 (Atlanta), Marcella Robertson with WUSA 9 News in Washington and WTVR 6 CBS station in Richmond.

"WUSA wanted us to come to DC for an "on the street" interview. We were already going up there for an Earth Wind and Fire concert so they said they would meet us at six o'clock at the corner across from Capital One Arena where the concert was being held.

"We had also gotten a call from a talk show host in California that wanted to do a Skype interview with us that afternoon.

"Micky Tingler was going with us to the concert so he agreed to drive. Here we were flying up I-95, Emma and me Skyping with the talk show producers, on our way to do an interview with a radio station on the street before an Earth Wind and Fire concert. It was crazy.

"We get to the street corner and there was a guy with a camera and wires and cables all over the concrete. The guy doing the interview was in the radio station; the guy on the street didn't know we were there to dance too. It was messy. We were tripping all over the cables. That's where I said I had more steps than the Washington Monument. Problem was, I didn't do a very good job showing them."

A few days later, a good friend, Steve Jarrell who lived in Nashville, happened to be visiting friends in Fredericksburg. Steve did a *Daddy-O on the Patio* radio show in Nashville and interviewed Nick and Emma for his show from a small studio in Fredericksburg.

What excited Emma most when *Southern Living* did a short article on them. She has always enjoyed their recipes.

"When they (people) see us dancing, they see what we feel. They see the love on the floor and how close we are together," Nick said during the *Southern Living* article.

Nick and Emma were also invited to do a guest performance at an Animal Shelter fundraiser.

Within days, they received a call from another talk show host to interview via Skype. They didn't make the cut with the first host, but after two more interviews with the second, they were invited to be on the show. It had to be kept a secret until their appearance, and because of a *Guest Release & Confidentiality Agreement*, the name of the host cannot be revealed.

Nick had a hard time getting off work from FedEx.

"They don't just let you off," he complained to Emma. "They want you there. I ended up having to tell the manager who decided it was a once in a lifetime opportunity and made an exception."

Emma was working at the OB/GYN office and simply said she needed to go out of town for four days.

Jaimie and Michelle went with them to California. They had to travel on three different flights and literally flew in one day, did the show the next day, then flew home. Jaimie said it was all a blur.

"They were the nicest people," Emma commented of the entertainer and producers. They paid for everything – the plane tickets, stay at the Hilton – one of the producers is a friend on Facebook.

"When the producers interviewed us at the studio, it was an all-day thing. They asked about our favorite show –

Dancing with the Stars – and tried to get Derek Hough on the show but ended up getting Val Chmerkovskiy as a surprise guest."

Nick and Emma were also asked the name of their favorite singer and Nick answered Bruno Mars. They were given tickets to a Bruno Mars concert in Washington, D.C. the following spring.

"That trip was an experience. We were there three days and two nights and with the help of Michelle and Jaimie, learned how to do Uber."

They saw the HOLLYWOOD sign and *Anderson's Observatory*. Went to the *Universal Studios* which was down the street from the Hilton but couldn't stay long as the Observatory was getting ready to close.

The four of them went to the *Hard Rock Café* and saw a few other clubs.

While there, they came upon a young man singing on a street corner. Nick and Emma stopped to dance.

"It was the most relaxed we have ever been in all our years of dancing."

~ From Jaimie. "Nick and Emma have inspired my life with their love for each other, sports, dancing to music.

"Their passion for dance has helped make their marriage last and earned them plenty of attention online."

Jaimie Ashton, Emma, Nick and Michelle at the Hilton Hotel in California.

Michelle, Emma, Nick and Jaimie. If you look close, you can see the HOLLYWOOD sign near the top of the mountain behind them.

Steve Jarrell, Emma and Nick.

MINI-STROKES

Nick lay in the hospital bed. Reached for Emma's hand and stared at the doctor.

"I understand you had a lively weekend," the doctor said. "Want to tell me about it?"

Emma looked at her husband. "Well, I guess you could say this has been building up." She squeezed Nick's hand. "Do you want to start at the beginning?"

Nick considered Emma's suggestion, then turned to the doctor.

"I guess it started last March when my arm swelled up a little at the Battleground Relays. But it went away. Then in October it happened again." Nick looked at Emma. "Remember, we were going to that Bruno Mars concert. We were driving across the Woodrow Wilson bridge and I said, 'Emma, my hand feels numb. Do you suppose it could be carpel tunnel?'"

The doctor looked at Emma. He knew she was a nurse.

Emma shrugged a shoulder. "I wasn't sure, but when it settled down and the feeling came back during the concert, we just sorta forgot about it."

"Yeah, the numbness went away again, and I didn't think any more about it."

"You never had any more numbness?" The doctor asked.

Nick shook his head. "Maybe a little, but it always went away. I just figured it was carpel tunnel."

"What was so different about this week?"

"This Wednesday, I got up at my usual time – three a.m. – to get ready for work. I ate a little breakfast then went into the bathroom to brush my teeth. I reached for the toothbrush, but it fell out of my hand."

Nick stared at his hand, flexed it.

"I remember looking at it, couldn't believe I'd been so sloppy. It took several tries, but I finally cleaned my teeth, then I sat on the edge of the bed and thought, 'if I can't hold a toothbrush, how can I sort packages at FedEx?'

"I sat there a few minutes and when the feeling started coming back, I decided to go on in to work. I got there and we were standing around talking like we normally do for ten or fifteen minutes. We have these stretching exercises we do before we start work and I couldn't put my hands behind my back. It was difficult but I finally managed it. I remember flexing my hands on the way to my station and told my supervisors, 'watch out for me. I might be going home.'"

"They didn't ask you why?" The doctor asked.

"I told them I wasn't feeling one hundred percent. They said to do what I could. I almost dance some while I'm working because several conveyor belts intersect at my station and I do a shuffle as I read the shipping labels and shift packages in the correct path. We always start a little slow so I could build up my rhythm but this morning, I was having trouble with my hands. I couldn't move fast enough.

Packages started to back up and I told myself, 'I can't do this. I need to go home.'

"I told my supervisors I was going home and went to punch the clock. I dropped the card. When I bent down to get it, I couldn't pick it up with my right hand. Finally had to pick it up with my left hand. One of my co-workers stopped and asked if I was okay."

"Did you go to a doctor?"

Nick shook his head. "I stopped at the CVS by the hospital and said my hands were numb. The assistant pharmacist came over and said, it seems like it could be more than carpel tunnel. I think he said something about rotator cuff. Said I should go to the doctor and have it checked out."

"Did you go to a doctor?" The doctor repeated.

"We called the doctor," Emma interrupted. "To rule out carpel tunnel. He had Nick do the Nuclear Stress tests on Friday. We haven't gotten the results yet."

"And you didn't rest over the weekend." the doctor studied Nick.

"No. We had plans for this weekend, and it wasn't bothering me as much. It was Mother's Day weekend and we had plans to go to Busch Gardens for some dancing. I was going to take Emma to Captain George's on the way home."

Emma's watched the corners of the doctor's lips curve upward.

"We left Saturday morning, stopped at a New York Deli on the way there," Emma said. "Nick ordered a Greek salad but didn't eat much. Said something didn't taste right."

"So, you went to Busch Gardens. How did you feel?" The doctor asked Nick.

"Like Emma said, something didn't set right with me. I didn't even feel like dancing a whole lot. Later that night, I did a lot of tossing and turning in bed. I'd lay on one side and it would go numb. I'd turn over and lay on the other side until that side went numb."

"He tossed and turned the whole night," Emma stated. "I'd been up since four, because of his restlessness."

"At six o'clock, I said 'let's go get breakfast.'" Nick said. "We took showers and I don't think they were serving breakfast that early."

"No, we were too early for the complimentary breakfast, but the receptionist served us some cereal and Danish. Half-way home, Nick remembered it was Mother's Day and wanted to go to Capt. George's. By now, I was concerned. I knew something wasn't right, and I wanted to get home."

"We were driving through King William, and pulled up to gas station, for gas and a bathroom break. I followed Emma inside and seconds after she disappeared into the bathroom, I just stopped in the middle of an aisle and froze. My mind went blank. I couldn't step forward. I couldn't step backwards. I just stood there like a freak. There was this little kid standing nearby, staring up at me. He asked me if I was okay and I couldn't move. I didn't know what to do.

"Emma came out of the bathroom and asked me what was wrong. I started stuttering and spitting...."

"He was so pale," Emma whispered. "I knew something was wrong. I helped him out to the car."

"Yeah, I reached to open the door and I couldn't pull it open. I looked at my right hand and it just curled up." He rolled his fingers into a fist to demonstrate what happened.

"That's when I knew I was in trouble," Emma said. "It was all I could do to get him in the car and race home. I was determined to take him to the first hospital we came to, but Nick said he wanted to go to Mary Washington. So, here we are."

"It appears that you had a series of mini-strokes," the doctor said. "We did an ultrasound to check for blockage in your carotid arteries, and it is about fifty percent. We don't normally want to do anything until it is at least seventy percent. Your heart rate is low, and we want to monitor that as well. We're going to send you home, but I want you to take it easy."

Michelle made a surprise visit home to visit. She couldn't afford a flight from Atlanta but a friend drove her to North Carolina where she met Micky Tingler who brought her to Fredericksburg.

Nick, Emma and Michelle made some administrative decisions and went to the bank to take care of the paperwork.

On the way home, Nick wanted to go to the *Firehouse Subs* for lunch despite Emma and Michelle's objections. While there, Nick had another episode but didn't want to go back to the hospital. They went to Primary Urgent Care who sent him to the hospital anyway.

Nick was in the hospital three different times over the next month for a brain scan and EKG's. He eventually had surgery on the carotid artery and has experienced no more incidents of numbness or slurred speech.

Everything seems to be back to normal and he and Emma are back to dancing.

Closing

Nick and Emma lead a much more relaxed life now. Lately, the calendar has been full of doctor's appointments, but that doesn't stop them from going to the gym to work out three days each week, the movies on Tuesdays and dancing every weekend.

"We've had a full life," Emma sighs, "but it's nice to take it easy too. If I could do it all over again, I wouldn't change a thing. I'd still be a nurse. I owe this to my mother, the Mary Washington Hospital teachers, Mrs. Jane Engles, Dorothea Dix, Phyllis Lippman, Laura Hatch and the many nurses that I worked with every day. That's how much they mean to me."

Nick smiles. "Doing this book has brought back fond memories. Made me realize I've been blessed. The kids were so good. They were like sponges – they absorbed whatever I tried to teach them. Working with all those athletes was important. And inspiring. One success in your lifetime is good but I had three of them – James Eberhardt, best single performance; Micky Tingler strongest lifter and Colin Dwyer best thrower. And that's just the tip of the iceberg."

Michelle keeps their *Nick and Emma The Dancers* Facebook page updated with their activities. Recently they attended a benefit for a homeless shelter, *Loisann's Hope House,* at Dodd's Auditorium at Mary Washington University and saw Bill Medley of the *Righteous Brothers*. It was a very memorable evening for Emma who videoed a lot of the songs on her cell phone.

They spent one week in Myrtle Beach and one week in Atlanta, celebrating their 50th wedding anniversary with Michelle and her family in September, 2019. *Paul's Bakery* provided a cake to them.

Anywhere they go, Nick and Emma see familiar faces. People comment, "remember me? I used to come to your Nickel Gym."

They recently won the "Cutest Couple married 50 Years" sponsored by the Free Lance-Star and won a gift card. They won the "Cutest Couple married 25-49 Years" the previous year.

Emma continues to cut her eyes at Nick and smile her crooked smile. "I fell in love with Nick's personality, not his looks. When we dated, he proved to me with his kindness and willingness to listen to people, even giving some in need money, that he was the man I wanted in my life. He has made me the happiest woman in the world. Without him, I would never have visited the places we have seen, met the people we have met, or done all we've done over these fifty years. I can't express the gratitude for the loving friendship we share."

Nick often kisses Emma on the cheek and says, "She's the rock that makes me roll."

"They say marriage is 50/50," Nick goes on, "and yes, it is so, but during all the years of track and field, football, dancing, raising our daughter, working, we would never go to bed mad. We'd talk it out, say I love you, and share a kiss. Never stop saying I love you. Work together and always keep the communication open. Things happen in life you can't control. Live each day to the fullest and hope for the best."

Nick still hasn't participated on "Dancing with the Stars" but dancing with Val Chmerkovskiy is a good exception. And being singled out by Chubby Checker isn't bad either.

Nick always has a twinkle in his eyes, a broad smile on his face and is happiest when he's on the dancefloor with Emma.

Once he noticed two young couples watching them as they danced. As he and Emma were getting ready to leave, Nick stopped to talk to them.

"We just like watching you two dance," one of the girls said. "My husband and I want to be like you when we grow up."